A Gift
Renewed

"...you delivered to me five talents;
here I have made five talents more."
(Matthew 25:20)

A Gift
Renewed

The First 25 Years
of The University
of Michigan-Dearborn

1959-1984

Elton D. Higgs

The University of Michigan-Dearborn
DEARBORN

International Standard Book Number: 0-933691-00-9
Library of Congress Catalog Card Number: 85-50432
The University of Michigan-Dearborn, Dearborn
© 1985 by The University of Michigan-Dearborn
All rights reserved
Printed in the United States of America
Second Printing

To my colleagues at The University of Michigan-Dearborn,
by whose talents I have been enriched

Contents

Foreword

Twenty-five years is not very old for an institution. After a quarter of a century most institutions are still considered in their infancy. But accumulated years and maturity seldom are correlated. The University of Michigan-Dearborn illustrates this point very clearly. After just a quarter of a century the campus has matured and, in our considered judgment, functions with maturity as well as efficiency and productivity very convincingly.

The rapid maturity of the campus can be attributed to several factors. Chief among these are the executives from the several divisions of the Ford Motor Company and The University of Michigan whose vision of the campus was so clear that translating vision to institution could readily be accomplished. Equally important, perhaps, have been the dedicated faculty and staff who did whatever they had to do—especially in the early years—to nourish and nurture the fledgling campus. Their dedication, inventiveness, and belief in their work cannot be overestimated.

The campus was built on the very stable foundation of more than 150 years of University of Michigan experience, tradition, and dedication to excellence. It did not have to chart a course in unexplored waters.

The original mission of the campus has been pursued, and that mission, though now augmented, is generally followed today. The liberal arts programs and course offerings, especially in the freshman and sophomore years, have necessarily come to occupy a more prominent place at UM-D than in the beginning, but a major and significant role is still given to off-campus, experiential learning; the option in cooperative education, for example, is now offered in the College of Arts, Sciences, and Letters (CASL), as well as in the Schools of Engineering and Management, and other kinds of internships have developed also. It is a mark of its maturity that UM-D has fulfilled the spirit of its original design without remaining a single-purpose institution. The national experience with such limited institutions has been that they do not flourish.

One other lesson has been learned nationally: upper-level institutions are not viable or economical. UM-D, like the other eight or ten experimental campuses in the country, had to add programs for the first two years after 12 years of offering only upper-level and master's degree programs.

In looking back over the 25 years one finds three distinct periods in the campus's metamorphosis: (1) the initial period (1959-71) when the campus was small, offered upper-level and a few master's courses, and reached an enrollment plateau; (2) the period of rapid growth and expansion (1971-1980) when the enrollment increased about 500 percent, four new buildings were built and others were planned, and the liberal arts component quickly came into clear prominence; and (3) the period which began with the State of Michigan's most severe recession (1980-1984) during which time the 1981 peak enrollment basically was maintained but many other features of the campus were consolidated or down-sized.

The future character of the campus is difficult to project. So much depends on the fortunes of the State of Michigan and its view of its responsibility to higher education. But in choosing a theme for the 25th Anniversary celebration we chose our words very carefully: "Celebrating 25 Years of Building for the Future." Whatever challenge the future brings, the campus is willing to face it; and whatever way UM-D can serve public higher education in Michigan, it is willing to undertake. The record shows it can play a vital role, and it hopes to.

On behalf of my colleagues on the faculty and staff, I express sincere appreciation to Dr. Elton Higgs, professor of English, for so ably chronicling the first 25 years of The University of Michigan-Dearborn. He reported in a style that revealed the task was a labor of love.

WILLIAM A. JENKINS
CHANCELLOR

Preface

Three previous treatises have dealt with the history of UM-D: "A History of the Development of the Flint and Dearborn Branches of the University of Michigan," a U. of M. dissertation written by Sharon Campbell in 1973; parts of a book by Robert Altman, *The Upper Division College* (San Francisco: Jossey-Bass, Inc., 1970); and a U. of M. graduate paper, "A Brief History of the University of Michigan-Dearborn, 1956-1981," by Barbara S. Zitzewitz. Although I have consulted these works, I have relied primarily on newspaper clippings, memos, letters, and official publications available in the UM-D Library Archives and in the Bentley Historical Library at the U. of M. in Ann Arbor. I have also listened to a number of taped interviews with people connected with the early years at UM-D. Most of these were conducted by Mr. Herschel Wallace, the first director of student affairs for the campus, and are housed in the UM-D Library Archives; a few were conducted by Ms. Sharon Campbell and are housed in the Bentley Historical Library in Ann Arbor.

The first of several appendices to this history is a "List of Principal and Key Documents" relating to the development of UM-D. A few of the most important and interesting ones are reproduced in Appendix Two of this book; others are available in a supplementary Xeroxed volume of "Important Documents in the History of UM-D," which will be placed in the UM-D Library.

I should make it clear that in this treatise I am attempting only to survey the evolution of UM-D as an entire institution over the past 25 years. I shall not, therefore, be giving much attention to developments in individual units, except as these may have affected the campus as a whole. Certainly each unit, both academic and non-academic, has a story that needs to be told in detail, and I would have liked to tell it; but time and space will not allow that degree of specificity in this volume. I have, however, included in my "Chronology of Events and People" (Appendix Three) many events relating to the individual units, and I have noted all of the unit heads over the years in "Selected Tables of UM-D Personnel and Units" (Appendix Four).

My thanks are due to the 25th Anniversary Committee and to Vice-Chancellor Eugene Arden and Chancellor William Jenkins of The University of Michigan-Dearborn for appointing me to this task, as well as for reading and calling my attention to errors in the manuscript and making it possible for the book to be published. I must also thank those people whose memories of former stages of the campus and whose interest in this project have enriched my research. Mr. Herschel Wallace, the first director of the Office of Student Services at UM-D and director emeritus of the Office of Registration and Records, helped me to delve into the UM-D Archives, which he established, and he gave me access to some of his personal files as well. Prof. Emeritus Emmanuel Hertzler also gave me materials from his personal files. Prof. Dennis Papazian, presently director of graduate studies at UM-D and a veteran faculty member and administrator on the campus, made some helpful suggestions on the manuscript, as did Dean Victor Wong of the College of Arts, Sciences, and Letters at UM-D. Other readers whose responses were helpful were Profs. Sidney Warschausky, Bernie Klein, and Christopher Dahl and Dr. Donn Werling, Director of the Henry Ford Estate-Fair Lane.

Although I must acknowledge the limitations of this little treatise, I am mindful of my mother's frequent statement when guests sat down at her dinner table: "Well, apologies are no good to eat, so I'll not offer any." Neither, I think, are they good fare for readers; so I will merely express the hope that those who read the account of how the Fair Lane Estate of Henry Ford became a successful campus of the University of Michigan will find that their time has been as well spent in reading it as mine has been in writing it.

ELTON D. HIGGS
JANUARY 18, 1985

A Historic Moment
U of M President Harlan Hatcher and
Ford Motor Company President Henry
Ford II on the lawn at Fair Lane after
the December 17, 1956 announcement
of the Ford gift to the University of
Michigan. *Ford Motor Company*

1
Introduction

September of 1984 marked the beginning of the 26th year of operation for The University of Michigan-Dearborn, which opened as the Dearborn Center of The University of Michigan on September 28, 1959. This volume chronicles the development of the campus from its inception as a joint project by the Ford Motor Company and The University of Michigan, through its early period of low enrollment and its subsequent expansion, to the present period of its maturity as an established, diversified, fully accredited unit of The University of Michigan serving the Detroit metropolitan area.

The first movement toward what was to become The University of Michigan-Dearborn began with some studies of manpower supply conducted by Mr. Archie Pearson, director of training for Ford Motor Company, in the middle 1950's. He was convinced that serious shortages were looming for the Company in qualified, college-trained engineers and junior administrators. Accordingly, he made discreet inquiries of educational institutions in the Detroit area concerning their willingness to adjust their programs to meet these needs. Pearson was particularly interested in a program with a cooperative education component which would provide several periods of full-time work experience, alternating with regular terms of professional academic study. According to Pearson (as stated to interviewer Herschel Wallace in 1979), his enquiries and those of his associates did not strike the responsive chord they were looking for until they were put in touch with members of the top administration at The University of Michigan. Thus in late 1955 began the negotiations between Pearson, his associates Arthur Saltzman and Hoyt Anderson, and University of Michigan officials Marvin Niehuss (executive vice-president), Harold Dorr (dean of statewide education) and Harlan Hatcher, president of the University, which led to the establishment of the Dearborn Center of The University of Michigan. During 1956, the details of the proposed campus were worked out

Top left: An early class at the Dearborn
Center. Top right: Interning in the 1980's.
Philip T. Dattilo Bottom right: Interning as
an environmental consultant. *Philip T.
Dattilo* Bottom left: An early student dance
on Fair Lane's terrace. *Joe Van Mill*

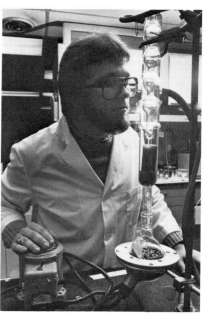

by a Special Committee involving top administrators at both Ford Motor Company and The University of Michigan. The announcement on December 17, 1956, of a gift of land and capital development money from the Ford Motor Company to The University of Michigan made it obvious that the focus of the agreement between the two was the building of an upper-division and master's level campus of the University which would adopt the cooperative work-study requirement as a part of its regular degree program in engineering and business administration. The University was to provide the regular professional and liberal arts courses necessary to a University of Michigan bachelor's or master's degree, with the co-op work assignments forming an integral addition to the regular academic requirements.

The upper-division cooperative education program, then, was the first important educational emphasis of what is now The University of Michigan-Dearborn. Cooperative education is still a vital part of the professional programs of UM-D, and not only has it expanded during the last 12 years to include liberal arts students, but other kinds of off-campus experience for credit have been added as well. There are now regular program-related internships in political science, economics, social work, humanities, health sciences, and public administration. Nevertheless, it became apparent in the early days that the campus could not afford to be limited to a single focus, and over the years it has (though not always with as much premeditation as could have been desired) gone through several stages of modifying its original purposes and structure.

From its inception in 1956 to about 1962 (the Center's fourth year of operation), the cooperative education program was confidently set forth as a sufficient *raison d'etre* for the campus, in spite of growing evidence that this admittedly fine and educationally sound opportunity was not drawing a sufficient number of students for economical use of the facilities. In February 1962, William Stirton, the University of Michigan vice-president who was the first chief executive of UM-D, announced that cooperative education was being extended to the liberal arts areas on an optional basis, beginning in the fall term, 1962. Specific reference to the availability of liberal arts co-op assignments was made in the general section of the Dearborn Center *Announcement* for 1963-64, but the section for the Division of Literature, Science, and the Arts makes no mention of it at all, and there were very few liberal arts co-op work assignments actually made before 1973, when the present liberal arts co-op program was officially established. Although this early abortive attempt to extend the co-op program to liberal arts was an apparently small episode in the history of the campus, it constituted the last major attempt to build the campus solely on the basis of the co-op programs and the upper-division/graduate structure. Moreover, it came at about the same time as the change in the name of the institution from "Center" to "Campus" (to make its objectives seem less limited). Both events seem to have marked the beginning of a period in the middle sixties characterized by growing uncertainty about the future of the institution. This period ended in 1969 with the recommendations of the Ross Committee (also referred to as the Balzhiser Committee, and officially called the Dearborn Campus Planning Study Committee), which radically changed the direction of the Campus.

The 1969 report of the Dearborn Campus Planning Study Committee, appointed by University Vice-President for State Relations and Planning Authur Ross to consider the future of the campus, recommended the adding of the first two years and the expansion of non-co-op programs; they recommended other changes as well, most of which were implemented in 1971 to give the campus its present structure. It became at that time a four-year undergraduate institution (newly designated "The University of Michigan-Dearborn") with a continued commitment to some master's level graduate programs, having a chancellor as its chief executive officer; two years later, the old divisions became schools and colleges, and the Division of Education ("Urban Education" for the first few years) was created, with each of the major academic units headed by a dean.

After that watershed change in 1971, UM-D grew rapidly from just under 1,000 students to over 6,000 in 1979. During this period there was a scramble just to supply the courses and facilities needed to accommodate the soaring student population. New faculty were added at the rate of 10 to 20 per year, and the face of the campus changed as a whole new set of buildings was planned and constructed, mostly to the south of the original buildings. But this period of expansion was brought to an end by the decrease in the pool of students (nationwide as well as locally) and the economic recession beginning about 1980. There ensued a period of great budgetary difficulty from which the campus is finally, in 1984, feeling the first stages of relief. So UM-D is ending its first 25 years of operation in an attitude of realistic optimism.

The successive stages of UM-D development, then, coincide roughly with five periods, from the preparations for its establishment to the end of its first quarter of a century of existence. Accordingly, this account of the history of The University of Michigan-Dearborn will be presented in chapters corresponding to these five units of time:

1955-1959: Background and Planning
1959-1963: The Cooperative Experiment
1963-1969: Reassessment
1969-1979: Expansion
1979-1984: Consolidation

The mere relating of events, however, will not do justice to either the human idealism or the human foibles that contributed to the formation of UM-D over these years; so in the process of retracing our steps, I will glance from time to time at some of the personalities who are worth remembering, too.

Finally, throughout this brief history I will be concerned with the ways in which the benevolent beginnings of UM-D have been altered and renewed, through both designed and unanticipated events. I think that the sum of these changes and renewals will be viewed, both now and later, as positive, and that The University of Michigan-Dearborn will not be judged to have squandered the generous gift by which it was founded.

The First Construction
Vice-President and Dean William E.
Stirton (left), the first chief executive of
the Dearborn Center, in front of the
soon-to-be Classroom and Administration
Building. *Michigan Historical Collections,
Bentley Historical Library, The University
of Michigan*

2
Background and Planning 1955-1959

For information on the events leading up to the beginning of negotiations between Ford Motor Company officials and members of the University of Michigan administration concerning a possible collaborative educational effort between them, we must rely on information given by Messrs. Archie Pearson, Hoyt Anderson, and Arthur Saltzman, all of Ford's Training Department. All three (in interviews with Herschel Wallace, retired director of student services at UM-D) tell of their studies in the mid-fifties which revealed that Ford Motor Company would not be able to hire locally all of the engineering and business graduates that it needed. Pearson, the director of the Ford Training Department at that time, tells of his efforts in 1955 to see whether local institutions of higher education, particularly Wayne State University, would be interested in expanding into a cooperative education program to supply additional professional and technical graduates who could be recruited by Ford Motor Company. By the last half of 1955, there had been no response from these local institutions adequate to move Pearson to continue pursuing his objectives with them. Consequently, when he perceived through conversations with his friend, James Lewis (a former school administrator in Dearborn who had become the U of M vice-president for student affairs), that The University of Michigan might have some interest in his ideas, the way was clear for quick progress.

Negotiations for Ford Gift

Informal talks between Pearson and his associates and President Hatcher and several other U. of M. administrative officers led to their formal recommendation to the Ford Motor Company Administration Committee on January

Top left: The University of Michigan Regents at Fair Lane, spring 1957. Top right: Preparing the site, spring 1958. Bottom: Inside the Engineering Laboratory Building looking toward the Student Activities Building. *All Michigan Historical Collections, Bentley Historical Library, The University of Michigan*

11, 1956, that the Company negotiate exclusively with the U. of M. to see if a mutually satisfactory arrangement could be worked out. The Administration Committee accepted the recommendation, and a Joint Planning Committee was appointed, consisting of (for Ford Motor Company) John S. Bugas, vice-president for industrial relations; I. A. Duffy, vice-president for the Tractor Division; Charlie Moore, Jr., vice-president for public relations; Ray H. Sullivan, vice-president and group executive; and Arjay Miller, controller; Pearson, Saltzman, and Anderson assisted this group, and Mr. Robert S. Dunham, general industrial manager, was often the Company's contact person for the negotiations. Representing the University were Harold M. Dorr, dean of state-wide education; Marvin L. Niehuss, executive vice-president; Harlan Hatcher, president of the University; and the deans of the Schools of Engineering and Business Administration. James Lewis, already mentioned, was present at several meetings of the joint group, and William K. Pierpont, vice-president for business affairs, was active throughout the negotiations.

The first meeting of this group was held at Inglis House, a U. of M. facility in Ann Arbor, on February 17, 1956. The year-long negotiations centered on detailed projections of curriculum, numbers of students in the several programs, facilities, and the number of graduates that would be suitable for the manpower needs of Ford Motor Company. Agreement on these matters was reached in July 1956, and on July 28 of that year another presentation was made to the Ford Motor Company Administration Committee with specific recommendations from the joint committee on the square footage of the buildings for the proposed campus and on the size of the gift for constructing them. The rest of the arrangements were primarily concerned with the legal requirements of Ford Motor Company in making the gifts of land and money. The projection of needs for the new campus and the negotiations for funding and establishing it were culminated in two official letters of request from President Hatcher to Henry Ford II, dated November 5, 1956, the terms of which had already been agreed upon: a gift of not less than 200 acres* of land from Ford Motor Company, preferably a tract including the Fair Lane Estate built by Henry Ford; and $6,500,000 from the Ford Motor Company Fund to build the campus. These two gifts were formally announced at the Fair Lane mansion on December 17, 1956.

Planning for the Center

The next step after the announcement of the gift of land and money from the Ford Motor Company and the Ford Motor Company Fund was to confirm

*It should be noted here that although from the very beginning, public statements reported the amount of land given by Ford Motor Company to be 210 acres (even 212 in some later accounts), the deed, which was not transferred to the University until October 1, 1957, shows the actual amount of land in the gift to be 202.59 acres. Because of two exchanges in land in 1967 and 1970, the present area of UM-D is a fraction over 200 acres.

acceptance of the responsibility for operational funding by the University of Michigan Regents and the Michigan State Legislature. The legislature took its initial step in a joint resolution by the House and the Senate on January 9 and 10, 1957, wherein they commended the Company and the University for their joint effort and recommended that the U. of M. Regents accept the proffered gifts. At its meeting in February 1957, the Regents officially accepted the gifts and the responsibility for developing the Dearborn Center. Planning for the physical development was undertaken even before the official acceptance by the Regents; in January, the University hired professional consultants to "study this project and prepare preliminary plans, specifications and estimates of cost."

Simultaneously, an academic planning committee was appointed to shape the curriculum and the administration of the new Center. A letter from Dean Dorr to the deans of Business Administration, Engineering, and Literature, Science and the Arts (LSA) on January 7, 1957, shows that the University administration's response to the Ford gift was immediate. In this letter, Dean Dorr specifies 12 areas of University commitment to Ford in the development of the Dearborn Center.

1) Sufficient facilities for the number of students agreed on (2,700)
2) Co-op programs in business administration and engineering
3) Junior, senior, and master's level courses only
4) Coordination with Henry Ford Community College for four years of integrated undergraduate work
5) Instructional staff equal in quality to Ann Arbor's
6) & 7) Degree programs comparable to Ann Arbor's
8) At least minimum student service facilities
9) Consider "quarter" system for academic calendar
10) Offer complete program in engineering and business administration each quarter
11) Consult with industry in planning and administering co-op programs
12) Secure adequate operating funds

Dean Dorr then goes on to outline certain tentative assumptions and some remaining questions to be answered by the University concerning the prospective programs at the Dearborn Center. "The sense of the discussions," he says, "indicated an intent to provide a full schedule of daytime courses in Engineering, Business Administration, and the Liberal Arts and Sciences." However, he continues, "except for Engineering and Business Administration where some preliminary studies have been made, matters of curriculum and educational policy remain in the realm of speculation." He refers to "other problems to which attention must be given, such as internal organization and overall administration, the relationship of the Center to the Dearborn community with special reference to the Henry Ford Community College, policy questions involving administrative relations with comparable campus units, educational standards, staff recruitment of assignment, etc." This letter, then, constitutes a program for planning the new center by the University and is essentially a charge to the planning committee, to which Dean Dorr is asking the three academic deans to make nominations.

The minutes of the Conference of Deans for January 9, 1957, show an extended report by President Hatcher and Dean Dorr on the status of planning for the Dearborn Center. Dean Dorr referred to his letter of January 7 and reiterated its principal points. Vice-President Pierpont then stated that Dorr was to serve as chairman of the "continuing Planning Committee for the Dearborn Center."

By February 13, nominations had been made to the Planning Committee by all except the School of Business Administration. Dean Odegaard of the College of Literature, Science, and the Arts had on February 1 set up an elaborate subcommittee from his unit, chaired by Prof. Edward L. Walker of the Psychology Department. In a letter of that date to Dean Dorr, Prof. Walker states: "To date we have had no opportunity to discuss over-all educational relationships with engineering and business administration or to discuss the implications for graduate school programs. I, therefore, request that you create the context within which it will be possible to discuss the liberal arts contribution, along with the contribution of other faculties, to the total Dearborn program." Dean Dorr accordingly set up a meeting of representatives from these units for February 18, 1957.

It is not clear why, but this joint group of the three academic units made no progress, and letters to Dean Odegaard from Prof. Walker on April 5 and May 15, 1957, indicate that a second attempt at joint planning, a steering committee on curriculum, was also unsuccessful. It appears that in the College of Engineering there was some objection to using the steering committee, of which Prof. Walker was to be chairman, as the means of planning the total curriculum of the Dearborn Center. As a result of these difficulties, the subcommittee for the College of Literature, Science, and the Arts issued an independent report of its conclusions on June 13, 1957. As we shall see later, this document, which was the only official planning committee report for the new campus, came to be rather influential in fixing the final structure of the Dearborn Center which was authorized by the Regents in January 1958.

Key recommendations of the "Walker Committee" (to name it for its chairman) were (1) that the Dearborn Center have a resident faculty equal in quality to, but independent of, the Ann Arbor faculty; (2) that a vigorous, creative, and experienced educator be appointed as dean of the Center as soon as possible, and that he be given full administrative authority for the Center, reporting directly to the president of the University and his executive staff; (3) that there be three academic "divisions": Liberal Arts, Engineering, and Business Administration, and that joint appointments and cooperation between faculty of these units be made as easy as possible; (4) that there be no program in teacher education and no liberal arts graduate programs at first, and that evening courses be provided by the University of Michigan Extension Service; (5) that the liberal arts curriculum of the Center not offer any courses usually considered as freshman/sophomore prerequisites, and that any introductory courses in liberal arts be directed specifically at more mature students; (6) that students should be admitted only after having completed 55 credit hours or more at the freshman/sophomore levels, including about two-thirds of their approximately 40-50 hours of distribution requirements; (7) that the Liberal Arts Division offer concentrations in 13 subjects, as well as courses without concentrations in three foreign languages and philosophy; and finally, (8) that the faculty be willing to experiment with innovative kinds of instruction, such as continuing instruction by all faculty in communication skills at the upper-division level, the institution of a cooperative work-study program in connection with liberal arts subjects, and liberal arts courses for executives.

Dean Harold Dorr, who had begun the process of specific planning for the Dearborn Center in January of 1957 and had seen it run aground, saw that the LSA subcommittee report could be used to reinvolve the other academic units and to produce some tangible results from the planning activities. After some prearrangements with President Hatcher, on October 31, 1957, Dean Dorr was appointed by Vice-President Niehuss to chair a top-level "Committee on Organization for the Dearborn Center," consisting of Dorr and the deans of Engineering, LSA, Business Administration, and Graduate Studies. This committee completed its work in less than three weeks and reported its recommendations on November 19, 1957. Part II of its report was the text finally adopted by the Regents as the section of the University of Michigan Bylaws establishing the Dearborn Center (1958 Bylaws, Chapter XXXIII).

The Dorr Committee recommended, in concord with the Walker Committee, that the dean of the Center have administrative independence from Ann Arbor academic units and that an executive committee be appointed to act for the faculty on important matters concerning the campus as a whole. The Executive Committee was originally constituted, however, so as to guarantee direct participation by the Ann Arbor deans of Business Administration, Engineering, and LSA in the affairs of the Center, each of them having the option to serve on the committee or to appoint a representative; the other three positions on the Executive Committee were to be filled by any U. of M. faculty member of Senate rank, recommended by the president and appointed by the Board of Regents.

The Dorr Committee also accepted the Walker Committee's suggested structure of three academic divisions for the Center and set up standing committees to govern each of the divisions; nevertheless, all three of the original division chairmen were regular Ann Arbor faculty who served only part time at Dearborn and eventually returned full time to the Ann Arbor campus (R. Lee Brummet, Business Administration; Axel Marin, Engineering; Karl Litzenberg, LSA), and "resident" faculty at Dearborn were not included in the standing committees until 1961. However, only one specific programmatic tie was preserved between Dearborn Center programs and academic units in Ann Arbor: the restriction that no "program of graduate studies may be authorized except in compliance with the rules and regulations covering similar offerings on the Ann Arbor campus." Moreover, graduate programs in Dearborn were normally to be under the jurisdiction of the Horace H. Rackham School of Graduate Studies.

The original bylaws governing the Dearborn Center also specified that cooperative education was to be an integral part of the campus's curriculum and degree requirements and that instruction was to be limited to the upper division and graduate levels. The Dorr Report was submitted to and approved by the Regents on January 10, 1958, and the Dearborn Center at that time became officially an academic unit of the University of Michigan.

Construction of the Dearborn Center (1958-59)

Preparation of the site of the new campus on the grounds of the Fair Lane Estate began in February of 1958 with the awarding of sewer, utility, and grading contracts; in April the vice-president for business and finance was empowered to negotiate with the City of Dearborn for water, sewage disposal, and police and fire protection, and the Regents awarded the general construction contract for the campus to Spence Brothers of Saginaw. On May 22, 1958, construction was begun with a great deal of publicity and a major statement by President Hatcher on the rationale and purposes of the Dearborn Center.

Hatcher said that the formation of the Dearborn Center has "been guided by two important considerations": (1) the integration of co-op assignments with the student's academic program, and (2) making academic quality the primary concern. He then went on to enumerate the advantages of cooperative education, in the liberal arts as well as in the professional units, making reference to the literary college subcommittee report by Prof. Walker. Among the advantages President Hatcher listed were the forging of a link between experience and theory in education, the enhancement of individual career planning, and the lightening of the financial burden of higher education for both students and institutions. He ended by citing a study showing that co-op graduates chose their careers more quickly, advanced more rapidly, were happier with their career choices, and tended to participate more actively in civic affairs.

It is clear from these comments by President Hatcher that the official position of the University at the founding of the Dearborn Center was that the campus was to be an across-the-board adventure in cooperative education, while at the same time maintaining uncompromisingly the traditional academic standards of The University of Michigan. The only cloud on the horizon of the new Center's future was a lack of adequate operating funds from the state legislature which might delay its opening until 1960. As to the educational plans of the Center, the President spoke confidently of its serving 2,700 students with a blend of academic excellence and practical experience that The University of Michigan had not tried before and that had seldom been achieved anywhere.

Construction on the Dearborn Center facilities continued through the summer and early fall of 1958, while the faculty planning the curriculum in Ann Arbor (particularly in Engineering) determined the equipment which would be needed for the laboratories, and the University Library ordered the first basic materials needed for the projected programs. Although a search for the chief executive officer (dean) of the new campus was also being conducted during most of 1958, the details of that search have not been documented, and it was not until October 1, 1958, that William E. Stirton was appointed director of the Dearborn Center, in addition to his existing appointment as a vice-president of the University. (The original intention of calling the chief executive officer at Dearborn a dean was implemented only during the three-year tenure of Norman Scott from 1968 to 1971; after 1971 the chief executive officer was called the chancellor.)

Stirton was in many ways an appropriate choice as director of the Dearborn Center, and he was in a position to smooth over many intra-University problems in the founding of the campus that an outsider would have had greater trouble with. He was also well acquainted with the Detroit area business and industrial community, having directed a job training program at Cass Technical High School in Detroit during World War II and being familiar with both political leaders and business leaders in southeastern Michigan. Moreover, he was completely committed to the cooperative education emphasis of the new campus and was indefatigable in setting forth the rationale and advantages of the University's making such a program available in the Detroit area. Indeed, it might be argued that he continued emphasizing cooperative education as the campus's central focus some time after it became apparent that a broadening of the institution's objectives was required if it was to continue to exist.

In March 1959, the first Executive Committee of the Dearborn Center was appointed by the Regents. It consisted of Prof. Algo Henderson of the School of Education; Prof. John Lederle, College of Literature, Science, and the Arts; Prof. Gordon J. Van Wylen, College of Engineering; and Deans Stephen Attwood, Roger Heyns, Russell Stevenson (replaced during the next year by Floyd Bond), and Ralph Sawyer, deans of the Colleges of Engineering and LSA and the Schools of Business Administration and Graduate Studies, respectively; the deans were to serve ex officio.

Other original staff members hired by Director Stirton before the campus opened were Herschel Wallace, director of student services; Robert W. Beecher, business manager; George Baker, manager of grounds and plant; Donald E. Vincent, head librarian; Robert E. A. Lillie, coordinator for work-study in engineering; and L. Joseph Crafton, coordinator for work-study in business administration. Four of the original support staff, Olga Kovton in the School of Management office, Lee Miglio in the Chancellor's office, Donald Haidys in the Engineering lab, and Peter Murphy in Safety and Security, are still at UM-D. By the beginning of the fall term, 1959, there were three faculty in the Division of Business Administration besides Crafton (D. Ross Cowan, Hadley Schaeffer, and John G. Hutchinson), two besides Lillie in the Division of Engineering (Howard Colby and C. W. Johnson), and only one permanent full-time faculty member in the Division of Literature, Science, and the Arts (Sidney Warschausky), since the limited appropriation for the Dearborn Center allowed only programs in business administration and engineering and a few liberal arts courses to be offered the first year. (Another faculty member, Chester Camp, was appointed to teach a full load of mathematics for engineers during the first year.)

Because of legislative tardiness in supplying sufficient operating funds for the center for 1959-60, the actual beginning of academic instruction in the fall of 1959 was in doubt until late May; and although recruiting of students was carried on in the spring of 1959 by Herschel Wallace and William Stirton, even the projection of 150 students for the first term proved to be too optimistic. It was something of an anticlimax to all of the publicity about the Ford Gift and all of the preparation for a noble experiment in cooperative education that only 34 students were actually registered in the fall term 1959; but the structure of the campus was firmly in place, and optimism was still high that the original projected enrollment of 2,700 students could be achieved.

Faculty Remembered
Early faculty member Carl Cohen of the
Literature, Science, and Arts Division,
who was noted for his dynamic
speaking style.

3
The
Cooperative
Experiment
1959-1963

All of the publicity attending the opening and the first few years of operation at the Dearborn Center of The University of Michigan made it clear that the central purpose and the distinctiveness of the campus centered in its requiring cooperative work-study in engineering and business administration curricula and in its offering instruction only on the junior and senior and first year graduate levels. The first Dearborn Center *Announcement,* however, also made it clear that there were to be liberal arts degree programs in which co-op assignments were not required. Herein lay the source of the tension which became increasingly significant during the first 10 years of the campus's existence, for while those programs which were at the core of the Center's stated purposes failed to draw the anticipated number of students, the liberal arts programs, and especially the teacher education courses, attracted the largest share of the total enrollment. During the first four years of the campus's operation, it was possible to give the benefit of the doubt to the results of the University's foray into upper-division cooperative education; but when the attempt to implement co-op as a major element in the liberal arts programs failed, it was clear that the significant but limited success of co-op in the professional areas was not enough to sustain the campus, and that the original rationale of this branch of The University of Michigan had to be modified.

The Initial Programs

Classes opened at UM's Dearborn Center on September 28, 1959, with 34 students enrolled in degree programs in industrial and mechanical engineering and business administration. Only two of the four campus buildings were open at the time, the Classroom/Administration Building and the Student

Top left: Close interdisciplinary relation-
ships: faculty David Emerson (left),
chemistry, and Calvin DeWitt, biology.
Top right: A name change from Dearborn
Center to Dearborn Campus in 1963.
Joe Van Mill Bottom: The courtyard, the
center of campus in the early days.
Lens-Art Photo

Activities Building; the Engineering Building and the Faculty Office Building were not yet completed. There were no liberal arts courses offered during the first term, and only a few scattered support courses in the LSA Division during the second term. The calendar on which the campus began was divided into quarters of 12 weeks each, but by the end of the first quarter the administration had decided to go to trimesters in order to be able to mesh with the beginning of the second semester at schools from which transfer students might come. Accordingly, an extra month of course work was inserted in January 1960 to fill out the first term into a semester, and the second term (four months—a trimester) began on February 8.

Several adjustments made during this first year of operation were undoubtedly attempts to bolster enrollments. The decision to change the calendar was made in November; in January the beginning of liberal arts programs in the fall term 1960 was announced; in March, teacher education courses and a program in electrical engineering were announced for the fall term. An open house was held on the campus on April 10, 1960, to acquaint the community with the new facilities and the programs available at the Dearborn Center for the next academic year. Although most of the new offerings were merely a filling out of what would have been offered had sufficient money been available in 1959, the new program in teacher education, by contrast, seems to have been a direct response to a perceived market of students who might help to fill the gap between projected and actual enrollments. Moreover, its being instituted at this time is the more notable in that it was specifically recommended in the Walker Report that the Dearborn Center *not* include teacher certification, lest it duplicate educational services already available at neighboring institutions. Nevertheless, this move turned out to be the most effective of all the measures taken to bring in more students, since about a third of the total student body was enrolled in teacher certification programs by 1965.

Whatever combination of factors brought it about, the daytime enrollment in the fall term 1960 went up to 211. Adding to the sense that the campus was full of new activity were the 30 or so courses offered at night by the University Extension Service at the Dearborn Center, which brought in about 500 students, along with another 150 who took non-credit courses offered by the University Center for Adult Education. Director Stirton regularly included these evening non-resident activities when he talked about the number of people being served at the Dearborn Center.

A number of people who turned out to be influential in the Center's development for a number of years were added to the faculty in 1960: Paul Trojan in engineering (early 1960); Cedric Fricke in Business Administration; Emmanuel Hertzler (also early 1960), Allan Emery, Alvan Obelsky, David Burks, Carl Cohen, John Dempsey, Lorne Finlayson, Fred Goodman, Carl Haag, and Paul Carter (the last three in education) in LSA.

Emphasis on Upper-Division Co-op

In a memorandum of "notes" about the Dearborn Center circulated by William Stirton (undated, but probably summer 1960), the director is somewhat apologetic about what might be regarded as "undue emphasis on the cooperative aspects" of the campus, but justifies that emphasis by the fact that the cooperative programs are a "relatively new experience for the University" and need more explanation than the "long-established" liberal arts tradition. He notes that the Literature, Science, and Arts Division (LSA) will be opening in the fall of 1960 and will be worthy in every way of the University of Michigan tradition from which it springs. He at first leaves open the question of whether liberal arts programs will participate on an optional basis in the cooperative education experiment, but later on in the four-page document, he includes liberal arts co-op among the plans for future developments at the Center. There are several other comments that came to characterize Stirton's view of what the campus was intended to be and how it ought to be viewed. For example, he emphasizes the fact that because of its need for more educated employees, industry "approached The University of Michigan" about the possibility of establishing a branch campus; that the University avoided a four-year undergraduate program at the Dearborn Center (as well as at the Flint Campus) in order to preserve a good working relationship with the community colleges in southeastern Michigan; that the setting of the campus is "perhaps our greatest asset" because it provides "maximum availability of prime internships in industry and in business" and because it is "a pleasant and spacious campus"; and finally, that "it is not necessary to make a choice" between education "for a good living and for a good life."

These were to be the themes that Stirton used in representing the Dearborn Center (later "Campus") throughout his 10 years at its helm. And for a few years it seemed that perhaps the new campus could be successful according to its original design and purposes. Public interest in the Center was still generally high for the first couple of years, particularly in regard to what would be done with the Fair Lane mansion. On May 15, 1961, a conference of business leaders and scholars (including historian Sir Arnold Toynbee and sociologist David Reisman) was held to determine the best use of the mansion by the University. There seemed to be a consensus that it should be used as a conference center, but the realization of that goal, even on a limited basis, was some years in coming. Meanwhile, the campus continued to operate much below the capacity for which it was built (2,700 students, 1,700 on campus at one time), and except for the interest in Fair Lane, it largely faded from public recognition. Whether or not the delay of the dedication ceremony for the Center until October 1961 indicated embarrassment on the part of the University, it would seem to have been strangely anticlimactic, coming two years after the opening of the campus and taking place in a context of only 328 students and perhaps around 50 faculty and staff. The "ghost campus" struggled on in this way through the mid-sixties.

Administrative documents for all of Stirton's years as director are hard to come by, since his papers were inadvertently destroyed by the UM-D Plant Department after his retirement in 1968. The remaining papers indicate that he clung to the goal of making the campus work according to the original design, particularly in regard to the cooperative education program. Accordingly, in February of 1962 he announced that co-op assignments would be made available to LSA students on an optional basis in the fall term of 1962. The Dearborn Center *Announcement* for 1962-63 includes in its "General Information" section a reference to a "work-study plan on a limited voluntary basis" for LSA students, but no reference is made to liberal arts co-op opportunities in the LSA section of the *Announcement* either this year or any subsequent year (although it is mentioned in some of the LSA brochures). Between 1962 and 1968, there are scattered references to liberal arts co-op and to a few LSA students being on co-op assignment, but co-op job placements in LSA seem to have been left up to the campus administration, interested students, and the business administration co-op coordinator, who made most of these isolated placements. It would seem that there was no significant interest among LSA faculty at this time in exposing their students to the co-op experience.

Events of 1963

Several other developments converged in 1963 to make it a significant year in the campus's history. The most obvious and lasting of these was the change of name from "Dearborn Center" to "Dearborn Campus," the new designation being justified as more appropriate to a free-standing unit of The University of Michigan. The LSA Division first offered summer classes in 1963, indicating that it had recovered from starting a year behind the other two divisions and was coming into its own. (By fall term 1963 LSA was clearly the second largest division; by fall 1965 it was the largest.) The first graduate program at UM-DC, in mechanical engineering, was announced in 1963, finally adding a level of work that had been intended to be available from the beginning. There was a big push by the Regents and President Hatcher, bolstered by a volunteer citizens' "Committee for the Development of Fair Lane," to raise money for the refurbishment of the mansion ($250,000 was the goal). Official tours of the mansion were conducted for the first time by an auxiliary fund-raising group called the "Women's Committee for Fair Lane" in 1963. Only the auxiliary group had any significant success (it raised over $30,000), but even it disbanded after a falling out with the University administration over the accounting arrangements for the funds the women had raised (see Page 29, Chapter 4).

The year 1963 saw a subtle change in the way the "Dearborn Center" was regarded and in the way it saw itself. The change of name may be taken as symbolic of this alteration, although the "Dearborn Campus" came into being completely without fanfare (in fact, many of the signs around the campus didn't change until several years later). By 1963 it had become clear that extending the co-op program to liberal arts would not provide that division with a central focus, as it had with the professional divisions, and that a large proportion of the students at the campus had (and would continue to have) educational objectives which did not include cooperative work-study; and it was increasingly suspected that more students could be attracted at the freshman level than at the junior/senior level. Moreover, the LSA division was becoming restive at not having its own identity and mission, apart from the mission which sprang directly from the goals for which the campus was founded. The sufficiency of William Stirton's (and President Hatcher's) vision for the campus was increasingly challenged from 1963 on.

One might say that the first four years of UM-D's existence was its period of innocence. Everyone was united in trying the new concept of cooperation between industry and The University of Michigan. Because there were so few students and faculty during this early period, the universal testimony of those who were on campus at the time is that a very close relationship developed between faculty, staff, and students, and that classes and consultations alike were infused with a sense of adventure and challenge. Students were mature, well-motivated, and ambitious, and many of them alternated between full time work in the business and industrial communities and full terms in the classroom; consequently, professors found themselves dealing with active, informed, and critical minds. Faculty and staff alike felt a personal responsibility for the students, and students felt free to deal with faculty as mentors and advisors, rather than as absolute authorities. Faculty regularly consulted with colleagues in quite different fields, and disciplinary lines could be crossed freely.

Some of these early advantages of the "Center" survived for a few years after 1963, but by 1964, a student newspaper editor was already lamenting (with a student population of 617) that whatever student-faculty intimacy may once have existed was rapidly disappearing (*Ad Hoc*, December 21, 1964). Whatever the objective validity of his observation, the year of the first name change for the campus may conveniently be taken as a dividing point between a period of experimental "honeymoon" with upper-division cooperative education and a period when the original bases of the campus were being questioned and its very existence was threatened. Ironically, some of the founding notions of the campus were to prove their validity only after the basic structure of the institution was altered.

Student Protest
Dramatizing opposition to the proposed
separation from The University of
Michigan in 1968 with a mock funeral
at the Dearborn Campus.

4
Reassessment
1964-1969

Evidence that there were pressures for the Dearborn Campus to revise its original program is seen in the public refutations undertaken by Vice-President Stirton and President Hatcher, within two days of each other in February 1964, to squelch rumors that UM-D was about to expand to include freshmen and sophomores. The matter had been raised by a request from a committee of citizens in Flint that The University of Michigan consider expanding Flint College, the other U. of M. upper-division branch campus, to a full four years. Stirton gave an emphatic "no" to a question asked about whether the Dearborn Campus also was considering adding the first two years (*Michigan Daily,* February 26, 1964), and he was reinforced by President Hatcher a few days later (*Michigan Daily,* March 1, 1964). But these statements did not end discussion of the matter, especially among faculty members of the Literature, Science, and Arts Division at the Dearborn Campus, whose faculty meeting minutes reflect an increasingly intense concern with expansion during the middle 1960's.

Recriminations and Doubts

It was predictable that the LSA Division should feel restive about being limited to the two upper-division years, since the rationale for this limitation of the campus was so closely attached to the co-op program, which was not designed to place students in work-study jobs until their junior year. As we have already seen, LSA faculty were not committed to the focus on cooperative education which governed the establishment of the campus, and they wanted to use their increasing numbers to bring about a greater emphasis on developing a full range of liberal arts programs at Dearborn.

The chairmanship of the LSA Division was taken over in 1964 by John Dempsey, who was the first resident faculty member to hold that position, Karl

Top right: Arrival of U of M President Robben Fleming in 1968, a major turning point in Dearborn's fortunes. Bottom left: John Dempsey, first resident faculty member to be appointed chair of the LSA Division, later director of social services for the State of Michigan. Bottom right: Norman Scott, dean of Dearborn Campus from 1968 to 1971.

Litzenburg having held it since 1959 concurrently with his professorship in the Department of English in Ann Arbor. Dempsey was an aggressive politician who spoke his mind on behalf of LSA and argued for its unhampered growth. The faculty and administrations of the other divisions understandably defended the original design of the campus and regarded the burgeoning liberal arts programs as (to use an expression often heard in those days) "the tail that had come to wag the dog." Although UM-D is much larger and more complex now, some of those tensions have remained through the years, and a number of the faculty in business administration and engineering still voice regret that the campus is not regarded primarily for its excellence in professional co-op programs, and that liberal arts programs are so much in the majority.

There was also some ambivalence among the faculty at UM-DC about the campus's association with the University in Ann Arbor. From 1964 to 1969, a "second wave" of new faculty was recruited, and more of these came from institutions outside the Detroit area than was the case with the faculty of the first few years. Like the "third wave" of faculty recruited in the seventies, during the period of rapid growth, those who were hired in the sixties were drawn to a great extent by UM-DC's close association with The University of Michigan. Therefore, although the Dearborn faculty in the sixties, especially in LSA, wanted to be free of artificial controls and limitations exerted by the Ann Arbor administration, they also wanted to be recognized as University of Michigan faculty and wanted the campus to be supported by the University as an integral part of the U. of M. structure. Consequently, another tension developed within the system: at the same time that Ann Arbor's interest was waning in its "unsuccessful" stepchild, the faculty at the Dearborn Campus was crying out to the University for support and direction.

This feeling was forcefully expressed by John Dempsey in a long letter to Allan Smith, vice-president for academic affairs at The University of Michigan, on December 2, 1964 (LSA Administrative Files). Dempsey was speaking for the whole campus when he said that the Dearborn Campus's difficulties at that time were a result of "the inadequate level of financial and other support which this campus has received from Ann Arbor since its inception." He voiced the conviction that "the University has never really faced up to the existence of the Dearborn Campus, and has never resolved to develop it as it should." In looking at the history of the campus, he noted that it "commenced with an extremely modest operating budget" and that it has never "been given more than a minor proportion of its financial requests or needs."

For its part, the Ann Arbor adminstration found it difficult to justify continued support of the campus in view of the still-low enrollments, and Vice-President Stirton was always on the defensive about those enrollments. In a memorandum he sent to President Hatcher, dated May 2, 1966 (Hatcher Papers, Bentley Historical Library, Ann Arbor), he spends three pages answering a question asked of the president by a member of the state Senate Appropriations Committee. "Simply stated," Stirton says, "the question was, 'Why has not the Dearborn Campus of the University grown more rapidly?'" Stirton's answer identifies several deficiencies in University support that had hindered growth at Dearborn: lack of on-campus housing, lack of a full-time public relations person, the absence of a student center, the need for a new library, and lack of support for expanding programs in the liberal arts and establishing new graduate programs in every division. All of these, he concludes, "boil down to the simple need of money."

But Stirton's and others' pleas seemed to fall increasingly on deaf ears, or at least inattentive ones. The last part of Vice-President Stirton's tenure as director at Dearborn saw the retirement of those top adminstrators in Ann Arbor who had been responsible for negotiating the founding of the Dearborn Center—President Hatcher, Vice-President Niehuss, Dean Dorr—and the departure of many who had come from Ann Arbor to become the first adminstrators and staff at the Center. All of the original division chairmen and the original head librarian were gone by 1964, and Business Manager Robert Beecher and Plant Manager George Baker left in 1965. Stirton seems thus to have been somewhat less influential during his last years as director, although he continued to speak of and for the Dearborn Campus in the same terms as he always had. His message throughout his tenure at UM-DC is well conveyed in an article published in 1964 in a book called *Experimental Colleges* (ed. W. H. Stickler, Florida State University Press). In this article, Stirton extolled the co-op program at the Dearborn Campus as a way to combine preparation for both a "good living *and* the good life" (Pages 107, 118-119), and he focused on cooperative education to explain both the origin of the campus (as a response to industrial needs) and the continuing major purpose of the campus.*

Departures and Arrivals

A review of events which occurred between 1964 and 1969 shows that in spite of the uncertainty that surrounded the campus's future, there were pockets of activity that exhibited a vital concern among faculty, students, and staff with the creative use of existing resources. On the other hand, some steps were taken during this period that marked a break with the "old" campus and the assumptions on which it was operated. Of particular note were some of the personnel changes (including Stirton's resignation and the appointment of Norman Scott, of which more will be said later). Two of the original leaders in the physical

---

*That these intense convictions about cooperative education at Dearborn were not shared by LSA faculty was vividly demonstrated to me when I was interviewed for a position at UM-DC in January 1965. I was told by a prominent member of the Division that I would be talking to Vice-President Stirton a bit later, and that I should just discount his rhetoric about the centrality of cooperative education to the purposes and development of the campus, because the LSA division was not governed by such restrictive practices.

and fiscal management of the campus who left in 1965 have already been mentioned: George Baker, manager of plant and grounds, and Robert Beecher, business manager (who, incidentally, caused great surprise shortly before he left by suddenly marrying one of the secretaries on campus). Donald Klaasen began as business manager in February 1966, and he rose to a position of great influence in the operation of the Campus as Norman Scott's assistant dean.

John Dempsey took a leave of absence in 1966 to run for a seat in Congress and he never again assumed full-time status on the Dearborn Campus. He did, however, continue to be a friend of the Campus during the several years he served in the Republican state government, first as director of the budget and then as director of state social services. Dempsey died in 1982.

Two still-notable campus staff members were appointed during the late sixties. Edward Wall, who resigned as head librarian at UM-D in August 1984, was appointed to that position in the fall of 1967; he was the driving force behind the long, hard battle to get a new library built, and he has been a major positive influence over the years in making UM-D a center for chamber music and art exhibits. Another new appointee (1968) was Burton Harrison, assistant to the dean and then assistant to the chancellor, and finally director of institutional analysis just before his retirement in 1982. Harrison was known for his quiet, dry wit, and he could often be seen "making his rounds" of the campus to talk to people and see what was going on. He was an exceedingly versatile man; his background was in engineering, but he loved and read the Latin classics in the original, and on the side he was UM-D's first fencing coach.

There were several developments involving Fair Lane mansion during these years. In 1966 the public tours of the manison were stopped, and it was to be eight years before they were resumed, after the campus expansion was underway. Also in 1966 the Women of Fair Lane, a volunteer group which had conducted the tours and in other ways had raised money since 1963 to refurbish and restore the house and grounds, ceased its activities after a disagreement with U. of M. administrators over how their money was to be handled (about $36,000 by that time); they closed accounts in June 1968 by donating an original sculpture by Marshall Fredericks to stand in the small pool in the English Garden. Only recently have volunteer efforts on behalf of Fair Lane (under chairperson Peggy Campbell) reached—and exceeded—the accomplishments of the Women of Fair Lane.

Nevertheless, the mansion continued to receive attention. In May 1967 it was declared a National Historical Landmark. During June and July of that year a music festival was held in Jensen's Meadow in the hope that it would become an annual event, but it failed because the outdoor facilities were inadequate. In April 1969 the U. of M. Alumni Club of Dearborn presented the first of the "Evenings at Fair Lane," an arts festival which is still an annual event. The next year, the Fair Lane Music Guild was established, and its excellent chamber music seasons in the mansion have also continued to the present.

The most important change during the period 1965-1969 was, of course, the resignation of William Stirton as director of the Dearborn Campus. His departure, along with the retirement of President Harlan Hatcher, removed the last two barriers to a wide-open consideration of the options for UM-D, including especially its expansion into the first two undergraduate years. But the period while this deliberation was being undertaken by the Dearborn Campus Planning Study Committee (hereafter called the Balzhiser Committee, for its chairman) was not a happy one for the campus. The man appointed to succeed Stirton was an associate dean in the School of Engineering in Ann Arbor, Norman Scott, who served as dean of the Dearborn Campus from 1968 until 1971, when Leonard Goodall took office as the first chancellor. Scott had no experience administering a diverse campus like that at Dearborn, nor did he adjust readily to the tensions that this diversity occasioned. His style of administration was probably no more autocratic in reality than Stirton's, but he lacked Stirton's stature and reputation and his genial ability to smooth things over. It was perhaps predictable that he would find it easier to create a bureaucratic oligarchy with the business manager, Donald Klaasen, than to govern by negotiation. Whatever his abilities for the job, he was generally seen by the Dearborn Campus faculty and the academic adminstrators as ineffective and insensitive to their needs (see comments by faculty in Campbell, Page 254, and Zitzewitz, Pages 16-17). During this crucial period of transition for the campus, the academic units struggled especially against Donald Klaasen, whom they perceived as a tyrannical business manager-turned-assistant dean filling a power vacuum at the top of the campus.

Campus Planning Study Committee

The major turning point in the fortunes of the Dearborn Campus came as a result of the appointment of Robben Fleming as president of The University of Michigan in January 1968. He came to the position after having served as chancellor of the Madison campus of the University of Wisconsin, so he knew the dynamics of a multi-campus system. He showed his interest in the Dearborn Campus by making a visit there in October 1967, even before he was officially appointed as president. During that visit each of the divisions at Dearborn prepared a report for him, outlining their present status and objectives. He recognized the need for an immediate analysis of the Campus's problems and potentialities and for the setting of another direction for its future. Fleming directed his new vice-president for state relations and planning, Arthur Ross, to form a special committee to study the Dearborn Campus and to chart its future. Vice-President Ross formed his committee (called the "Dearborn Campus Planning Study Committee") in November 1968; it consisted of Dean Scott, Professor Paul Carter, and a student, Thomas Bagott, as representatives of the Dearborn Campus; Dean Stephen H. Spurr (Rackham Graduate School) and

Professors William Porter and Richard Balzhiser (who chaired the committee) from the Ann Arbor campus; and James Ford and Leonard Sain from the Detroit metropolitan community. The committee made its report in May 1969, and its recommendations created the biggest stir on the Dearborn Campus since its founding, finally changing its basic structure and propelling it into the only boom period it has ever known.

The key recommendations of the Dearborn Campus Planning Study Committee were that the freshman and sophomore years be added and new graduate programs be allowed to develop; that facilities be built to accommodate an eventual expansion to 5,000 students; that co-op be made optional in all divisions, but that a special effort be made to implement it as a fully live option in LSA; that the name and structure of the Campus be changed and the support level be radically increased so that it could become independent from The University of Michigan after five years; and that the campus direct its programs toward constituencies appropriate to its urban surroundings, creating to that end a citizens' advisory board which is "broadly representative of the metropolitan area."

The direction charted by the Balzhiser Committee was largely the one taken in the next 10 years by the Dearborn Campus; two years later, the campus had a chancellor and 313 students in its first freshman class, and the enrollment of 5,000 students projected by the committee for 1980 was exceeded in 1976, reaching over 6,000 by 1979. The Regents approved all of the committee's recommendations except those connected with the separation of the Dearborn Campus from The University of Michigan. Indeed, the committee had been charged to do its work on the assumption that UM-DC would "remain an integral part of The University of Michigan," but the committee saw no reason that that arrangement should be permanent and was even of the opinion that the campus was not likely to come to full development if it remained a part of the University. It was this recommendation that created the most controversy.

Although in its approval of the Balzhiser Committee recommendations the University of Michigan Regents did not endorse the concept of a "spin-off" of the Dearborn Campus, the Michigan House of Representatives Committee on Colleges and Universities held a hearing in the Multi-purpose Room of the Campus to discuss a bill introduced by Representative George Montgomery which would have separated UM-DC from The University of Michigan as "Fairlane University." Students and faculty alike turned out to protest the bill, but it was the students who dramatized their opposition by parading across the campus carrying a casket representing the death of UM-DC if the separation was carried out. Students also made the most of the initials of the proposed name on their placards.

Representative Montgomery responded to the protests by saying that he had introduced the bill primarily to call attention to the fact that The University of Michigan had not provided sufficient support to UM-DC as a branch campus to enable it to reach its legitimate potential. The implication was that if the association of the Dearborn Campus with The University of Michigan was a hindrance rather than a help, the campus might do better to go its own way. At any rate, the bill was not passed, and the campus threw itself into preparing for the admission of freshmen and sophomores on the assumption that both students and faculty would continue to be attracted to UM-DC because of its offering a University of Michigan degree, with the attendant quality and prestige appropriate to that degree.

On November 11, 1969, The University of Michigan-Dearborn campus formally celebrated its 10th anniversary. Its first decade had been marked by the frustration of a much heralded experiment in education, concentrating on cooperative education at the upper-division level while strenuously maintaining the top quality of all programs according to University of Michigan standards. As was so often emphasized by Vice-President Stirton, UM-DC was designed to provide education for *both* a good living and a good life. These ideals were noble and were sincerely held by many who saw the Campus through its first years, especially in the professional Divisions of Business Administration and Engineering. By the mid-sixties, however, the campus was under severe pressure to raise its enrollments, and it was clear that operational financing for the noble experiment was not forthcoming on the basis of idealism alone. Consequently, as a result of the Balzhiser Report, the Dearborn Campus was poised in late 1969 on the brink of the new direction it was to take in the 1970's; using its excellent co-op experience, its solid faculty, and its high-quality programs as springboards, the Campus initiated an expansion that transformed its atmosphere and appearance, increased its ties with the surrounding metropolitan community, and established it as a major unit of The University of Michigan.

Making History
Dean Norman Scott with the first two
freshmen admitted to the Dearborn
Campus in 1971, William Williamson
and Laura Gawronski.

5
Expansion
1970-1979

Soon after the Balzhiser Committee Report, and even before the Regents formally accepted the Committee's recommendations in November 1969, preparations were underway at the Dearborn Campus for the admission of a freshman class. The Campus's Executive Committee established in August of 1969 both an Ad Hoc Faculty Committee on Freshman Admissions and a Freshman/Sophomore Curriculum Committee, each of which reported early in 1970. In material prepared for Gov. William Milliken when he visited the Dearborn Campus on November 24, 1969 (only three days after the Regent's approval of UM-DC's expansion), the target date for the first freshman class was given as "the fall of 1971." Furthermore, several moves were made almost immediately to implement some of the administrative and fiscal recommendations of the Dearborn Campus Planning Study Committee: the process of separating UM-DC's budget and legislative appropriation from Ann Arbor's began in 1969 (although it was not officially listed separately until 1971); the Dearborn Campus Graduate Board was created in October 1969; a Chancellor Search Committee was appointed in May of 1970; and the first Citizens' Advisory Committee was appointed in 1970. Nevertheless, in spite of this apparently fast start, there was a good deal of scrambling to get courses prepared, laboratories built, and faculty and staff hired by September 1971; and the nagging problem throughout the 1970's—sometimes overshadowing the exhilaration of adding new students, staff, and programs—was the lack of adequate space, usually because of insufficient funding from the state.

Early Preparations and Appointment of a Chancellor

Although the first chancellor of "The University of Michigan-Dearborn" (the official name of the campus since April 1971) was not appointed until July 1971,

Top left: First Alumni Society Board in
1973: l to r (front) Carolyn Hawkins, Len
Suchyta, Emil Birdsong; (back) Pauline
Slebodnik, Wayne Tourda, Michael
Teeley, Ron Papke, Joan Schloop. *Joe Van
Mill* Top right: Leonard Goodall,
chancellor of UM-D from 1971 to 1979.
Bottom: Michigan Governor William
Milliken (third from right) and the first
UM-D political science interns in
fall 1971.

a great deal of activity took place on the campus during 1970 and the first half of 1971 which meshed with or paved the way for expansion. Some were academic developments: in January 1970 a new Bachelor of General Studies Degree was instituted by the LSA Division; in August of that year, the North Central Association gave UM-DC its first accreditation independent of Ann Arbor; and Prof. Robert Smock was appointed to a temporary position as academic co-ordinator for the campus in September 1970. In February 1971, the second graduate program in engineering, an M.S.E. in electrical engineering was begun, having been passed through both the new Dearborn Graduate Board and the Rackham School of Graduate Studies in Ann Arbor.

Several of these developments in the year before the first freshmen came were directed at refining UM-D's contacts with the surrounding area. In October 1970, U. of M. President Robben Fleming appointed a citizens' committee to study the relationship of the Dearborn Campus to the community around it. In the same month, in order to bolster the recruiting of the hundreds of students who would be coming to the expanded UM-D, Jack Petosky was appointed as the first separate director of admissions for the campus. On October 18, 1970, the Fair Lane Music Guild, which over the years since then has become one of the major cultural organizations in Dearborn, held its first concert, having been founded during the preceding months by three UM-D staff members, C. Edward Wall, Richard Reynolds, and Sidney Warschausky. In the summer of 1971, Prof. Orin Gelderloos conducted the first of several summer environmental workshops for Detroit area high school teachers with the help of grants from the National Science Foundation.

The new chancellor was announced in late February of 1971, but the naming of Robert H. Maier, vice-chancellor of the University of Wisconsin at Green Bay, proved premature. In less than three months, Maier notified the University that he could not accept the appointment, and the choice among the finalists had to be made again. This time Leonard E. Goodall, vice-chancellor of the University of Illinois at Chicago Circle, was selected, and he began his tenure on July 1, 1971.

Leonard Goodall (he was known as "Pat" around the campus) meshed very well with one of the major recommendations of the Balzhiser Report: that the Dearborn Campus establish itself firmly as an urban-oriented campus, creating programs and educational methods that reach out to business and industry, non-traditional students, and minorities. Goodall was a political scientist with a particular interest in metropolitan government and urban problems. His earliest public statements, therefore, reinforced the "urban" image of the campus. In the *University Record* of October 25, 1971, he is said to find "an urban environment…both attractive and challenging," and he is quoted further as saying, "In urban universities, people come together from a wide variety of academic, economic and ethnic backgrounds. Campuses such as UM-D must build upon this diversity as a part of the educational experience." Specifically, according to the article, Goodall wanted to "expand [UM-D's] traditionally strong cooperative education concept to include students in sociology, political science, and the hard sciences." In his inaugural speech in January 1972, he said, "I hope that the concept of out-of-the-classroom, off-campus educational opportunities will become a major thrust of the academic program in Dearborn"; and he backed up his admiration for diversity in institutions of higher education by focusing on "heterogeneity" as the chief goal of UM-D.

Chancellor Goodall was not to find it easy, however, to guide this expanded campus along a unified path; although a liberal arts co-op program was established with the help of a federal grant by the winter of 1974, it did not attract a large number of students, and neither did the several successful but limited academic internship programs established during the seventies (seven were listed by 1979). Moreover, the highly qualified new faculty brought in by the expansion (especially in the College of Arts, Sciences, and Letters [CASL], where the majority were hired) were mostly oriented along more traditional, theoretical lines. They wanted to establish excellence in their own disciplines, and many had considerable trouble with the idea that the campus should be shaped primarily in reference to its industrial and urban neighbors. Indeed, a great many of them found Ann Arbor a more compatible place in which to live and to establish community ties than any area close to Dearborn. The ambivalence of being both The University of Michigan and the *Dearborn* campus was to continue to be felt. Nevertheless, it is this tension between its need to present an image appropriate to its metropolitan setting and industrial origins, on the one hand, and its underlying drive for academic quality, on the other, that has contributed more than anything else to the survival of UM-D. Without a sincere and at least somewhat successful attempt at reaching out in non-traditional ways to the community around it, the campus would probably have found it impossible to convince those who funded it that it was distinctive enough to be continued; but without its deserved reputation for academic quality, it would not have attracted the large number of students (and faculty) who have come to it out of respect for its being a unit of The University of Michigan.

Problems in New Construction

Chancellor Goodall's most immediately pressing problem, however, was the establishment of an orderly process of campus planning; so his first major appointment (in August 1971) was to make engineering faculty member Howard Conlon the assistant to the chancellor for planning. Conlon served in this pressure-packed position for three years, the climax of his efforts being the announcement in November 1973 of a $19,000,000 campus development plan worked out by a consulting firm, in which the main outlines of the construction that has subsequently taken place were first presented. Two of the key buildings in this plan, however, ran into funding problems: the University Library was delayed for five years, and the General Instruction and Laboratory Building (GILB; later GCLB) finally had to be shelved indefinitely in 1983.

Much of the needed space, therefore, had to be supplied by renovations and short-term or self-financed structures. The Classroom/Office Building (COB), opened in January 1973, was the first to be completed. (It was financed by state funds but was said to be a "temporary permanent" building.) In the summer of 1973 the first of many temporary modular units (there were about 30 by 1977) were brought in and attached to the Student Activities Building. The Recreation and Organizations Center (ROC) was finished in June 1975, although it was not so named until the following February. Major renovations to the Engineering Building (supplying new laboratories and large lecture halls) were completed by fall 1975. Other buildings—the Parking Structure, the Fieldhouse/Ice Arena, and the University Mall, all completed between 1976 and 1979—were financed through loans based on the prospect of special income from the use of the buildings.

But the key building to the expansion, the one mentioned consistently from even the mid-sixties, was the library, which was not begun until 1978 and was not fully occupied until the end of 1980. The delays and the disappointments in the construction of the library (officially called the "Library and Learning Resources Building") were the focus of the frustrations suffered by those trying to build the expanded campus in the seventies. The first legislative action on the library was a vote by the State Senate in June 1972 to appropriate planning money for it; two years later the Regents approved the construction plans for the library, but the governor and the legislature balked at committing funds for it. In October of 1974, Chancellor Goodall cautioned that UM-D's growth was being threatened by proposed reductions in state funding to higher education, especially in funds for capital development; nevertheless, in March of 1975 both the library and the GILB were excluded from capital development funds appropriated to UM-D, even though the governor had this time recommended the appropriation. By November of 1975, UM-D officials had to admit that development on the major items in the $19,000,000 building program had come to a halt. For the next two years there were attempts to fund the library through the selling of bonds authorized by the state, but to no avail. A state task force even recommended in late 1976 that UM-D restudy the feasibility of the projected library and consider sharing new library facilities with Henry Ford Community College. Chancellor Goodall firmly rejected this suggestion in a public statement of January 1977, in which he chastised the state for its two-and-a-half-year freeze on this vitally needed piece of capital development. Not until June of 1978 was UM-D authorized to take bids on the library; ground-breaking to begin its construction was on October 17, 1978.

It seems that during this period of frustrating delay, from 1973 to 1978, the only entirely satisfactory new building at UM-D was the purple martin bird house, donated by craftsman Ewald Seiter for Jensen's Meadow at Fair Lane in January 1976; and even that was a reconstruction, incorporating what was salvagable from Henry Ford's original bird house modeled on the old Pontchartrain Hotel in downtown Detroit.

Academic Changes During Expansion

In spite of the difficulties of creating enough space to accommodate the expanded number of students, faculty, and staff on the campus, new programs and curricula were devised and implemented at an almost dizzying pace. First were the changes and additions arising directly out of the Balzhiser Report: the basic courses for freshmen and sophomores and non-co-op alternative degrees in engineering and business administration. Afterward came new concentrations and degree programs spawned by the expertise and interests of the new faculty and by the need to supply more of the offerings consistent with the stated objectives of UM-D, including selected graduate programs.

The Freshman/Sophomore Curriculum Committee, consisting of representatives from all three academic divisions, the student body, and the library, made its recommendations in the spring of 1970. It sought to avoid the pitfalls of both over-rigid requirements and those with no coherence at all. It was openly conservative in trying to embody the traditional ideals of a liberal arts education, but the program it proposed was not exactly traditional, since it crossed disciplinary lines and required certain courses (such as "The City" and "Non-Western Culture") which covered areas not usually included in basic requirements.

The committee presented three categories of subject matter in which all students should gain basic proficiency: language, culture, and science, roughly corresponding to the traditional areas of the arts, the social sciences, and the natural sciences, respectively. In each of these three categories, there was to be a specified basic course followed by various options, some of which, like the basic courses, would also be specially created for the Core Curriculum. The basic courses were the Freshman Exploratory, which was a language skills course to be taught by faculty in all disciplines, using their choice of subject matter; Non-Western Culture, designed to "offset the normal ethnocentrism inculcated in most students"; and Matter, Energy, and Life, an interdisciplinary science course intended to give "a broad understanding of the nature of the physical universe and its relation to life."

There were some gaps in the coverage of the Core Curriculum, such as the lack of any explicit inclusion of the behavioral sciences in its requirements. But the most obvious slighting of a traditional requirement in this program was the relegation of foreign language to a position as only one of three options under the category of "Language." It must be conceded, however, that the foreign language requirement for graduation at UM-D had begun to erode even before the Core Curriculum was devised. Early publicity on the Bachelor of General

Studies degree program in 1970 was forthright in identifying the new degree as an alternative which circumvented the foreign language requirement. Although in the days when it was solely upper-division the Dearborn Campus required foreign language proficiency of transfer students before they could graduate, foreign language has never been an absolute, on-campus requirement for graduation at UM-D. Nevertheless, four foreign languages are now taught by six full-time faculty members and several part-timers at UM-D, and an encouraging number of students elect these courses as part of the relatively new program in International Studies, or as an option to satisfy distribution requirements, or merely as enjoyable and profitable free electives.

The Core Curriculum, as instituted in 1971 with the first freshman class, lasted only one year. There were several problems, but the most pressing was that the Freshman Exploratory was too expensive, being taught to sections of only 18 students by full-time faculty members; and the participation of faculty from all disciplines made it difficult to maintain consistent standards and expectations for the course. By the fall of 1973, a more conventional composition course had replaced the Exploratory as the core requirement, although the latter was still available as an elective. Several of the courses created for the Core Curriculum are still taught (Conceptual Mathematics; Matter, Energy, and Life; Western Culture), but by the fall of 1976 the general education part of graduation requirements at UM-D had been turned into an uncoordinated set of distribution options governed primarily by the organization of CASL departments. That non-integrated structure has remained to the present, with some variations in the several academic units. Interest in broad-based interdisciplinary courses has revived from time to time, especially in the present Honors Program administered in CASL; but the universal Core Curriculum at UM-D died in 1976.

In addition to three newly-approved degree programs which were already in operation by the time the first freshmen arrived (the Bachelor of General Studies degree in liberal arts [1970], the Bachelor of Science in Administration [non-co-op, 1971], and the new Master of Science in Engineering degree in electrical engineering [1971]), many other new programs and concentrations to accommodate the expansion of the campus came into being after 1971. The Professional Development Degree in Engineering (PDED), a post-baccalaureate program for professional engineers needing to fill gaps in their past education, was approved in 1972. Humanities, philosophy, and industrial and systems engineering were added as concentrations in 1973. Biochemistry, art history, music history, early childhood education, and physics appeared as degree programs in 1974. Companion concentrations in environmental science and environmental studies were also launched in 1974, the latter housed in the newest division, Interdisciplinary Studies (IDS), along with two other IDS concentrations approved in 1974: computer and informational science and urban and regional studies. The Master of Arts Degree in the Division of Education and the Professional Development Degree in CASL and Management were initiated in 1975. In 1977, the Master of Public Administration Degree (in IDS) and the extension of the M.S.E. to industrial and systems engineering were introduced. Finally, biophysical science, microbiology, and American studies were approved as interdisciplinary concentrations in 1978.

Besides all of the new degree programs, there were a number of special courses and other academic activities that characterized the "reaching out" of UM-D during this period.

1) The internship in political science, begun by Walter DeVries in 1971, continued to expand under Helen Graves, who took it over in 1973 and still heads it.

2) Emanuel Hertzler began the Office of Individualized Learning (now REACH) in 1974 and firmly established the use of self-paced audio- and video-taped courses as a part of the regular curriculum, with the aid of several hundred thousand dollars in grants from the Lilly and Kellogg Foundations.

3) Academic support services were provided for educationally disadvantaged students, especially minorities, through the Program for Academic Support (PAS), begun in 1973 under David McAllister as the Office of Special Support Services (not known as PAS until 1977) and continued from 1977 to the present by Maggie Martin.

4) The IGNITE program, providing for selected high school students to take college courses, was begun in 1975.

5) A number of scholarly conferences were held on the campus in the bustling seventies, covering such diverse subjects as creativity, medical ethics, and the monomythic hero. One of these, an international convocation on seventeenth century English literature originated in 1974 by Professors Ted-Larry Pebworth and Claude Summers, has become a biennial tradition in Fair Lane mansion; the sixth one was held in October 1984.

Organizational Changes

The first permanent new administrative position to be created after Chancellor Goodall took office was that of dean of academic affairs. A search committee was appointed to recommend a short list of candidates for this position in October of 1971, and it was filled by Eugene Arden in July 1972. The need for such a position had been recognized a year earlier with the temporary appointment of Robert Smock, a member of the sociology faculty, as academic coordinator. Prof. Smock stayed on as associate dean after Arden's appointment and assumed responsibility for the self-study of the campus required as preparation for a scheduled review of UM-D's accreditation status in 1974*

*A full 10-year renewal of accreditation for the campus's undergraduate programs was granted in 1974; graduate programs continued to be accredited through the Rackham School until the next accreditation review in 1984.

Dean Arden took responsibility for the development of academic programs and faculty in the expansion, while Chancellor Goodall addressed himself more to the problems of funding and construction, and to the building of an image for the campus.

From 1972 until the present, Eugene Arden has served UM-D effectively in this key position (now called vice-chancellor for academic affairs), from the boom days of the seventies to the budget-cutting agonies of the eighties. Having occupied a major administrative position for nearly half of the history of the campus, he has earned wide-spread respect for his integrity and his dedication. Much of the present health of The University of Michigan-Dearborn is a result of his long-term influence and encouragement.

In June 1973, the present organization of the academic units was instituted as a result of a set of new bylaws for UM-D which had been formulated during the previous year by a faculty committee and approved in the spring of 1973 by both the UM-D Faculty Congress and the Regents of the University. The new bylaws provided for the five major academic units now operating at UM-D: the Schools of Engineering and Management; the College of Arts, Sciences, and Letters; and the Divisions of Urban Education (the "Urban" part was dropped in 1977) and Interdisciplinary Studies; these were to replace the original three divisions of the campus. The new academic units were to be headed by deans; as it developed, the Division of Education was headed by an associate dean until 1984, and the Division of Interdisciplinary Studies (IDS) had no head but the chief academic officer of the campus for several years. The faculty member who assisted the vice-chancellor for academic affairs in administering IDS, Francis Wayman, became the director of the division in 1981. The schools, college, and divisions were to form departments for groupings of disciplines that seemed appropriate, each department to be headed by a chairperson. At the campus level, the former Executive Committee was replaced by two faculty committees, one to advise the chancellor (the Faculty Advisory Committee on Campus Affairs) and another to advise the chief academic officer (the Academic Affairs Advisory Committee). Acting deans were appointed for the new schools and the college for 1973-74, while searches were conducted for permanent deans; the present dean of the Division of Education, Richard Morshead, was appointed the associate dean of the division in 1973.

In March 1975, a significant step was taken in securing outside funds for research and academic development by the appointment of Lee Katz as the first associate dean of academic affairs for development and research support. She served until 1981, at first doubling as the coordinator of evening programs; but after July 1978, her full efforts were devoted to obtaining outside funding for academic activities, particularly for faculty research. Her office was the clearing-house for all faculty grant applications, and her efforts in this area produced, in 1978, the first million-dollar year in outside funds for UM-D.

She was an indefatigable worker, and, as anyone who has been the object of her persuasion knows, she was very effective in recruiting people to apply for the sources of support she uncovered; and after the applications had been made, she was equally effective in easing them through the complex machinery of funding organizations. Dr. Katz was succeeded in 1982 by Susan Burt, under whom the expansion of fund-raising activities has continued. In 1982 the name of the position was changed to director of sponsored research and development.

Several other changes in administrative staff and structure made in the seventies are important enough to mention, some because they involve people who have served UM-D in various capacities for a number of years, and others because they had a significant impact on the directions the campus took. One of the most interesting and successful of the administrative support personnel has been Virginia Sayles, who was a 1971 graduate of UM-D; she began her full-time administrative career as a special assistant to the chairman of the LSA Division in 1972, with particular responsibility for creating a liberal arts co-op program. She did so by obtaining three successive grants from the U.S. Department of Education to fund it. She took increasing responsibility for student advising and academic record-keeping in the LSA division (later the College of Arts, Sciences, and Letters), and was largely responsible for negotiating the "2+2" arrangements with community colleges, whereby their graduates with technical degrees are granted a full two years' credit toward a degree at UM-D. In 1979, she was appointed as regional director of the University of Michigan Extension Service at Dearborn, a position that a year later was entirely absorbed into UM-D's own structure as a result of the "divestiture" of the University of Michigan Extension Service's regional offices. In this capacity she has arranged a number of special seminars for business and industrial management personnel, actually earning money for the University during a period when it greatly needed such funds. In 1982, she added to her responsibilities the oversight of REACH, the unit that administers self-paced audio-visual courses for UM-D. Her energy and creativity, as student, administrative assistant, and director of various operations on campus, have greatly contributed to UM-D's success over the years.

Another person who began his career as an administrative assistant in LSA (in 1971) is Joseph Wright, who is now dean of student affairs. He took over the operation of student affairs (as director at that time) in the fall term of 1972 and presided over the expansion of non-academic student support activities that were so sorely needed as the number of students grew from hundreds to thousands. Some new student service personnel were already in place when Wright assumed the directorship: Nancy Hessler had served from 1970 to 1972 as the first director of student affairs; the first full-time counselors (Donald Brown, who now heads the Counseling Center, and David McAllister, deceased) were appointed just before the arrival of the first freshmen, in August 1971; Richard Sypula (a 1971 UM-D graduate) became director of intramural sports in 1971; he is now director of student activities and organizations.

Donald Klaasen, who had been an assistant dean under Dean Norman Scott, had his title changed to director of business services under Chancellor Goodall; he left in the summer of 1973 for another job and was replaced in February 1974 by Richard Schwartz, who was called the director of business affairs. This position, along with Eugene Arden's, was made a vice-chancellorship in 1976 (Joseph Wright's position in student affairs became a deanship at the same time). During this evolution of titles and redefinition of positions, it also became clear that it was the chief academic officer of the campus, rather than the chief financial officer, who would be the "second in command." The budgetary process was greatly opened up under Chancellor Goodall, who created a Budget Priorities Committee, provided access to approved budget information, and brought about wider involvement in the creation of budgets.

Other administrative offices created during this period were the Personnel Office (1973), the Financial Aid Office (1974), the Office of Women's Programs (1975), and the Office of Institutional Analysis (1977). A director of the Natural Area (Prof. Orin Gelderloos, who still holds the position) was officially appointed in 1974. In 1978, Chancellor Goodall established a group of Dearborn community leaders called the Dearborn Round Table to carry on regular discussions of matters of common concern to the University, Henry Ford Community College, and the City of Dearborn.

Other Developments During Expansion

With the increase of the size and population of the campus, UM-D began to be more visible and to draw more people from the community into its activities. The construction of the Fairlane Shopping Mall in 1973-76 brought a major improvement in access to the campus when two new entrances were opened off the new section of Evergreen Road between Hubbard and Michigan Avenue in the fall of 1976. When the shopping mall itself opened in 1976, the number of people seeing the campus of The University of Michigan-Dearborn merely by driving past increased dramatically.

There was, however, a sacrifice of some land by the University because of the developments around it. After intense discussions with Ford Motor Land Development Company officials, who wanted the University to contribute 10 acres at the northeast and southeast corners of its property to accommodate the extension of Evergreen, University administrators and the Regents reached an agreement with Ford to exchange land with the corporation at a sacrifice of only two acres; as a result, UM-D now has about eight acres at the intersection of Hubbard and Mercury Drive. Although the old Ford Estate gatehouse on Michigan Avenue was not on University land, some UM-D personnel joined community people in urging the Ford Land Development Company to preserve it; nevertheless, it was finally torn down in spite of vigorous citizen protests.

A number of public events and programs at UM-D in the 1970's drew people from the outside. With the increase in the campus's athletic activities (e.g., varsity soccer, 1974; varsity hockey with the Mid-Central Collegiate Hockey Association, 1977) and the opening of the Fieldhouse/Arena in the summer of 1978, more people attended sports events on the campus, both those of the University and those of groups renting the facilities.

Cultural activities blossomed during the expansion years. Besides the Fair Lane Music Guild, which had begun in 1969 but continued and grew during the seventies, the UM-D Cultural Events Committee, formed in the early 1970's, sponsored and arranged many free concerts on campus and, sometimes in cooperation with the Office of Student Life, kept up a steady flow of films and lectures that were publicized and available to the community. A drama group was formed at UM-D in 1974 and has given regular performances since that time, although in 1982 the faculty position in theater was dropped because of budget restraints. Perhaps the group's most successful performance in the period of expansion was *When You Comin' Back Red Ryder?* in November 1976 with Prof. Susan Flierl directing; but it had to be performed at facilities off-campus because UM-D did not have (and still does not have) an adequate theater auditorium. An attempt was made to solve this problem in 1975-76 in cooperation with Henry Ford Community College and the City of Dearborn, and indeed, a formal proposal was made to the U. of M. Regents by Chancellor Goodall and HFCC President Stuart Bundy in April 1976; but the objectives of the three groups proved to be too divergent, and HFCC began constructing its own theater auditorium in November of that year. (The City of Dearborn has not yet built a municipal auditorium.)

The Henry Ford Estate-Fair Lane has always been an attraction for the citizens of Dearborn, and the period of expansion provided more opportunities than ever before for the curious to visit the former home of Henry Ford. Chancellor Goodall, with the help of a number of volunteer guides (including Lois Goodall, his wife) responded in 1974 to community desires for access to the Fair Lane Mansion; it had been eight years since public tours were last conducted. The grounds were also made more systematically accessible and usable during the expansion years by the University's offering regular guided tours through the Natural Area. A trail guide brochure was made available in 1975, and a special Braille Trail was opened in 1976. In July 1977, Ford Motor Company gave a gift of $10,700 to finance a new brochure for the nature trails and tapes for the Braille Trail. Community groups continued to contribute to various aspects of the estate's restoration; perhaps the most notable of these services during the seventies was the planting of 800 rose bushes on the grounds by the Fair Lane Rose Society in June 1976.

With the expanding student body and the rapid increase in the number of graduates at UM-D, interest in a UM-D alumni group intensified. In November

1973, the first Board of Directors of the UM-D Alumni Society was elected, and the organization has been increasingly active since then. The first Alumni Day on the campus was in May 1977, when professors were on hand in specified areas to meet with their former students. Fund raising efforts directed at alumni began in 1977, and in 1983 over 600 of them contributed $35,000 to support special academic projects at UM-D. Graduates of The University of Michigan-Dearborn now number more than 10,000.

Overview of Expansion and Problems, 1971-1979

In 1974, in the fourth year of the expansion of UM-D, a "role statement" for the campus was approved by the Regents which stressed its commitment to "excellence with relevance"; this statement, in updated form, was reapproved in February 1977. With its stress on programs which have been traditionally strong at UM-D, such as co-op and other off-campus academic experiences, and on special provisions for minority and other non-traditional students in the metropolitan area, these role statements reflected and reinforced the statements made by Chancellor Goodall during his first year at UM-D. By April 1979, when he announced his departure from the chancellorship to take up the presidency of the University of Nevada at Las Vegas, the campus had grown by 5,000 students, had added 15 new academic programs and over 100 new full-time faculty members, and had constructed six completely new structures since the beginning of his tenure. There was a radical difference between the Dearborn Campus of the U. of M. in 1970 and The University of Michigan-Dearborn in 1979, and Leonard Goodall could be justly proud of the part he had played in that difference. By the end of his period in office, UM-D had come to be respected as a versatile and vigorous unit of The University of Michigan and was seen to be riding the crest of its successful growth. But the seeds of its problems during the next few years had already been sown. Some of the same forces that had brought on the economic difficulties of 1973-77 would regroup to hit Michigan even harder in 1980-83, when the automobile industry seemed to hit bottom and already-allocated state money had to be recalled. Goodall was fortunate enough to have left just before the latter storm broke.

The first years of expansion were heady stuff, even with all their problems. Bright young faculty members were given a chance to build a campus and to establish themselves as senior faculty in a comparatively short time, and the increments in budget and numbers of students each year from 1971 to 1975 seemed to be quite as much as the administration and staff could handle. By 1975, however, many of the new faculty had settled in enough to form a better idea of whether their goals could be realized by the patterns that seemed to be governing the growth of the campus, and the administration had concluded that the campus's growth needs would soon outstrip present and projected funding. Vice-Chancellor Arden said in his beginning-of-the-year report in September 1975, "There are two important constraints on our future growth. First, the state government is supporting our efforts at a *decreasing* rate per student, which would be difficult under any circumstances but is especially difficult during an inflationary period. In addition, we are nearly out of space." These constraints put a great deal of pressure on faculty who were trying to develop new programs, and instead of receiving increasing support, they found themselves with larger classes and fewer square feet per student for several succeeding years as the result of the stagnation of capital development which has already been described. Although the UM-D administration itself was chagrined at being denied much needed facilities that had at one time seemed very close to being funded, the faculty in 1977 felt the need to give their own voice to their frustrations by speaking directly to the University administration in Ann Arbor.

The "Committee on Faculty Concerns," as it was called at first, was formed early in 1977, and its first action was to prepare and send to all of the UM-D faculty a questionnaire to determine the level of faculty satisfaction with campus policies and facilities. The results indicated that the dissatisfaction overall was much higher than it had been four years before, when some of the same questions had been asked in connection with the self-study for the NCA accreditation review. Faculty discontent focused on inadequate facilities, over-loaded classes, insufficient or inept staff support for faculty, and the failure of faculty salaries to keep pace with inflation and with the rates of pay at comparable institutions. All of these concerns were voiced in a petition to President Fleming and the Regents in the summer of 1977, signed by 131 faculty members and requesting that the president and the Regents meet with the "Task Force on Faculty Concerns" and others appointed by the Faculty Advisory Committee on Campus Affairs "to discuss possible remedies."

All of this activity in 1977 points to some of the growing pains of the 1970's. It also indicates that the faculty hired in the expansion years identified enough with their new place of employment that they were willing to expend some systematic and constructive efforts (their final petition made it clear that they did not want to undercut Chancellor Goodall) toward the improvement of the campus. That kind of faculty involvement in the institution has been a basic reason for the continued high quality of UM-D; although the faculty and the administration (and sometimes different segments of the faculty) have often heatedly confronted each other, in the final analysis not only most of the faculty, but most administrators and support staff as well, have wanted the enterprise to succeed and have invested themselves in it. It is in the light of this kind of commitment by the majority of the UM-D faculty and staff over the years, and the good results produced by that commitment, that the lack of adequate financial support has so often seemed disappointing and discouraging. But as bad as the late seventies were, the worst was yet to come.

A Dream Realized
After a seven-year delay, a four-story
University Library at the new center of
campus. *Philip T. Dattilo*

6
Consolidation
1979-1984

The opening of UM-D's three new major buildings between 1978 and 1980 (Fieldhouse/Arena, University Mall, and University Library) marked the end of one set of troubles and the beginning of another: there was now an abundance of space, but not enough money to cover all operations. In the summer of 1979, the 10 modular structures on the northeast corner of the campus, serving the library and the CASL, General Services, and Personnel offices, were hauled away, to everyone's great relief. The SAB was vacated the next year, as the library moved into its new building and Hardee's restaurant was relocated in the University Mall. By April 11, 1981, when the new library was jubilantly dedicated, the population center of the campus had shifted to the new buildings.

But ironically, in that same month, probably the most painful short-term budget-slashing process in the history of the campus reached its culmination: a required $500,000 cut in UM-D's base budget to meet its share of Governor Milliken's call-backs of appropriated funds and to rebuild the campus's depleted emergency equity fund. The exhilaration at having finally acquired much-needed new facilities was greatly diminished by the difficulties of the next few years, which were climaxed by a three percent shortfall in faculty, administrative, and support staff salary raises in fiscal 1981-82. During the three-year period from mid-1979 to mid-1982, $1,121,513 was cut from UM-D's appropriated funds, and the effects of this traumatic retrenchment dominated most of the first four years of Chancellor William Jenkins's tenure on the campus, July 1980 to July 1984.

Chancellor Jenkins was appointed as the UM-D chief executive officer after a nationwide search during the 1979-80 academic year. He came to the position with wide experience as both an administrator and a scholar, having served as vice-chancellor for academic affairs and then as acting chancellor of the University of Colorado at Denver in the years just preceding his coming to

Top: The Fieldhouse/Ice Arena, a sports
facility opened in 1978, used by both the
campus and the community. Bottom: The
University Mall, opened in 1979, a new
hub for the campus. *Both Philip T. Dattilo*

UM-D, with administrative service at four other urban campuses before that. He had also served a year as president of the National Council of Teachers of English. All of his abilities and experience were to be severely tested, even during the first months of his tenure; but there were some bright spots, too, in this trying four-year period.

In spite of the difficulties of the years 1979 to 1984, UM-D has done more than survive. It not only received a 10-year maximum reaccreditation with commendations from the North Central Association of Schools and Colleges in July 1984, but it had individual programs in engineering, education, and chemisty accredited or reaccredited during this period as well. Moreover, UM-D administrators and the Office of Sponsored Research and Development have sought and received since 1980 a steadily increasing volume and range of outside financial support. And finally, The University of Michigan-Dearborn was able to end its 25th year with a gratifying 13.2 percent increase in its annual legislative appropriation for 1984-85, which, along with internal savings, enabled the administration to restore the three percent which had been cut from salary raises in 1981-82.

The University of Michigan-Dearborn began its 26th year with scars still visible from the experiences of 1979 to 1984, but the same spirit of persistence and professional integrity which has brought it through the perils of low visibility, underfunding, and insufficient facilities since 1959 is still in evidence, and UM-D's ability to provide first-rate academic programs to a wide range of residents of the Detroit metropolitan area has never been higher. The generous gift from Ford Motor Company by which the campus was established has been renewed repeatedly in its history through the redirection and reapplication of its resources; the course of UM-D's progress has sometimes been uneven, but the campus has not buried its talent in the ground.

Financial Developments

In one of his periodic newsletters to the campus community ("From the Chancellor's Desk," April 14, 1982), Chancellor Jenkins outlined the successive blows by which UM-D's budget had been battered since 1979: forced reductions of $101,275 in 1979-80, $591, 427 in 1980-81, and $299,403 in 1981-82, plus some indirect cuts, all adding up to 1.12 million dollars. In addition to these reductions in available funds, the campus had to assume the operational and maintenance costs of the new University Library and the University Mall when they opened in 1980. Consequently, in order to respond to the massive call-back of allocations from the state, money was taken from faculty and staff salaries, library acquisition funds, and various current accounts; open positions were frozen; and tuition went up by 13 percent, 22 percent, and 9 percent in successive years.

What made the financial situation especially difficult for Chancellor

Top: Chancellor William A. Jenkins who has guided the campus since 1980. *Philip T. Dattilo* Bottom left: Interim Chancellor Bernie Klein (left) in 1979, U of M President Harold Shapiro (center) and Professor Ted-Larry Pebworth at Fair Lane. *Randy McIntosh* Bottom right: Vice-Chancellor for Academic Affairs Eugene Arden, the first chief academic officer. *Philip T. Dattilo*

Jenkins was the fact that the budget for his first year (1980-81) was already $390,000 in the red, and only an emergency loan of $300,000 from the Ann Arbor campus, as well as severe economies, enabled the budget to be brought into balance by the end of fiscal 1980-81. However, by this time the campus's cash reserves were depleted, and President Shapiro mandated that sufficient cuts had to be made during the year to replenish this emergency equity fund: hence, the $500,000 cut in base budget during 1980-81. If this amount is added to the governor's call-backs, the cuts from 1979 to 1982 total over one and a half million dollars. It is not surprising that serious tensions developed within the UM-D community during this time.

The budget cut with the greatest emotional impact was the reduction of the salary package for the campus in 1981-82 to a level three percent below that given to faculty and staff at the Ann Arbor and Flint campuses. Although the chancellor had specifically alluded in an April 1981 faculty meeting to the possibility of a salary package for UM-D which might differ from that for the other two U. of M. campuses, the official announcement of a three percent raise for UM-D, contrasted with a six percent raise for UM-Flint and UM-Ann Arbor, was greeted by most UM-D faculty—especially in CASL—with surprise and consternation. On September 18, 1981, a strongly worded joint resolution from the CASL Executive Committee and the CASL Administrative Council (later endorsed by a majority vote at a CASL faculty meeting) was sent to all members of the UM-D Faculty Congress and to Chancellor Jenkins, who honored the CASL faculty's request that it be forwarded to President Shapiro and the Board of Regents. The resolution sharply criticized the salary package and accused the administration of not adequately exploring alternatives to such a drastic move.

Although the effect of the resulting confrontation was dissipated somewhat over the next few years, some strain in the relationship between the chancellor and the faculty continued. It was noted in the January 1984 Self-Study Report that "With the long-awaited turn-around in the state's economy and the improvement in the University's financial position, special efforts must be made by the administration and by the faculty to come into better alignment and cooperation with each other" (Page 190). Chancellor Jenkins put the restoration of faculty salaries as his first priority from September 1981 on, and his efforts bore fruit in July 1984, when UM-D was able to award a salary package for 1984-85 which was three percent higher than that at UM-Ann Arbor and UM-Flint.

There were also a number of other attempts by the UM-D administration to alleviate the campus's financial squeeze, both for the short term and for the long term, since it seemed obvious that legislative support for higher education in Michigan was not soon going to return to previous levels, if at all. In contrast to the high proportion of the total budget (75 percent) which was funded by state appropriations at the height of UM-Dearborn's growth in 1973-75, only about 52 percent of the total budget was funded by the legislature in 1982-83 (UM-D Self-Study Report, 1984, Page 14). Representatives from the UM-D

Citizens' Advisory Committee made a plea to the Regents for the special needs of the campus in November 1982, and Chancellor Jenkins augmented the staffing in the Office of Sponsored Research and Development so that efforts at raising money from outside sources could be stepped up. A major hurdle for the campus was to get itself included in the University of Michigan's overall capital fund-raising effort, the "Campaign for Michigan." Chancellor Jenkins and UM-D Sponsored Research and Development Director Susan Burt (appointed in June 1982) were able to accomplish this objective in July 1983, when the Regents gave their approval. Less than a year later, UM-D received its biggest capital gift since the founding of the campus: a grant of $800,000 from Ford Motor Company in May 1984 to build a computer-aided engineering (CAD/CAM) laboratory.

Efforts to encourage support from alumni were also intensified; $35,000 was raised from alumni in 1983, compared with only a few thousand dollars in 1977, when the first annual fund drive was conducted. In order to strengthen systematic and long-term contacts with UM-D alumni, Richard Reynolds, director of university relations, was appointed in 1983 to serve also as the director of alumni relations. Chancellor Jenkins also supplemented staffing in University Relations in order to improve the quantity and quality of public information about The University of Michigan-Dearborn.

Administrative Developments

Several significant administrative changes and organizational modifications were carried out between 1979 and 1984. Bernard Klein, the professor of political science and former comptroller of the City of Detroit who had been hired in 1971 to head the Center for Urban Studies, occupied the chancellor's chair in 1979-80 while the search for a new chancellor was being carried out. He was (and is) a man widely respected for his political acumen and experience. His first love, however, is teaching, and he steadfastly refused any administrative appointments that would take him away from the classroom, except for his one year as acting chancellor. Nevertheless, he accepted a special additional assignment from Chancellor Jenkins for 1984-85 to maintain a contact with the Michigan State Legislature and the governor's office on matters pertaining to capital development at UM-D. This duty was left unattended by the resignation in August 1984 of Vice-Chancellor for Business and Finance, Sal Rinella, who had functioned as the chancellor's governmental liaison. (Robert Behrens, head of accounting at UM-D, was appointed acting vice-chancellor for business and finance for 1984-85.)

Three notable administrative appointments were made in 1982. In April, Donn Werling, whose special interest was in historic preservation, was appointed the director of the Henry Ford Estate—Fair Lane, and he immediately set to work, as directed by Chancellor Jenkins, to obtain grants for the refurbishment of the estate and for the carrying out of the development plans for Fair Lane first presented in a professional report in January 1976 and updated in 1983. The second appointment, that of Susan Burt as the director of sponsored research and development, has already been mentioned. The third was of Edward Lumsdaine, the first dean of the School of Engineering recruited from outside the campus,* who was appointed in September 1982 with the express charge to develop outside research support for Engineering. He was very instrumental in obtaining in 1984 the $800,000 grant from Ford Motor Company mentioned above.

Two of the five major academic units obtained title changes for their chief executive officers during the early 1980's: Francis Wayman was made the first director of the Division of Interdisciplinary Studies in September 1981, and Richard Morshead, who had headed the Division of Education as associate dean since 1973, was made dean of the division in 1983. The Office of Institutional Analysis, after the retirement of Burton W. Harrison as its director in July 1983, was reduced in scope by the transfer of the financial analysis function to the UM-D Accounting Office in January 1984. Robert Smock, who established the Institutional Analysis operation in 1974, was appointed to serve on a half-time basis for 1984-85 as interim director of the now renamed Office of Institutional Research.

The use of computers for both administrative data processing and academic instruction increased dramatically at UM-D between 1980 and 1984. The first big breakthrough in the administrative use of computers was the completion of on-line registration procedures (using the Michigan Terminal System [MTS] in Ann Arbor) in the fall of 1980; at that time the long registration lines behind tables were no more. With the announcement in 1982 by the Ann Arbor administration that UM-D would no longer be subsidized for access to MTS, the UM-D administration began to take steps to boost on-campus computer facilities. Two new microcomputer labs were established for students (computer and informational science was the largest concentration on campus in 1984), and microcomputers were increasingly made available to faculty and office staff. Computer literacy began to be talked about as both a practical necessity and a possible academic requirement.

Academic Developments

The most basic academic developments during this period were the four recertifications received from accrediting agencies which were mentioned in the introduction to this chapter (NCA, ABET, NCATE, ACS). All of these accrediting procedures required extensive self-study activities which produced

---

*The search for a new dean of Engineering was begun in 1980, after the end of a 17-year tenure (the longest of any administrator so far at UM-D) by J. Robert Cairns as chairman and then dean of the campus's Engineering unit.

sizeable documents reporting on the condition of the units being eval-
uated. The most far-reaching of these accreditations was the one by the North
Central Association, which dealt with all academic and support units on the
campus, as well as UM-D's relationship to the overall University of Michigan.
The NCA Visiting Team was on the whole quite complimentary about the
quality of programs, students, and faculty; about the effectiveness of campus
administration and the positive attitude of support staff; about the improve-
ments in physical plant; and about the institution's restraint in not over extending itself in a period of limited resources. Most of the criticisms in
the NCA Team Report had to do with the effects of inadequate funding on
faculty and staff salaries, library acquisitions, laboratory and office space,
and equipment.

During the early 1980's, there was a renewed concern at UM-D for recruiting
and keeping exceptionally able students. The first UM-D Honors Convocation was held in March 1983 to recognize students who had distinguished
themselves academically during the past year, either by grade point average
alone or by receiving an academically based award. The faculty committee in
charge of the Honors Program, administered in CASL for all UM-D students of
sufficient academic standing, revised its guidelines in 1983, instituting a new
set of core honors courses (an interdisciplinary series on Western Civiliza-
tion) and encouraging faculty to create new tutorial seminars for honors
students.

In this period of financial stringency, new academic programs were very
selectively introduced. In the fall of 1980, the School of Engineering instituted a concentration in manufacturing engineering, toward which it had
received from Ford Motor Company a grant of $275,000 in March 1979.
In September 1981, the School of Management began its Master of Business
Administration degree, which by the end of the winter term 1984 was to
replace the Master of Management Degree. Although this is the first UM-D
graduate program not under the auspices of the Horace H. Rackham School
of Graduate Studies in Ann Arbor, it is coordinated with other M.B.A. degrees
in the University of Michigan system by a special committee appointed by the
President. The Division of Interdisciplinary Studies initiated a new undergraduate program in Health and Society which sprang from Prof. Marilyn
Rosenthal's summer travel courses on comparative health systems in foreign
countries. The most noticed new program between 1980 and 1984 was probably
the one begun in 1983 for Guest Scholars, which enabled senior citizens to
attend classes at UM-D at a greatly reduced rate of tuition. Younger students
in many classes were given the benefit of seeing things from the perspective
of people with great experience but still-active minds.

Support and recognition of faculty research efforts continued to be gratifying
in the early 1980's. The first mini-sabbaticals were awarded in 1979-80 through
the initiative of the vice-chancellor of academic affairs; these provided, es-

pecially for the young faculty, an opportunity to take off a full term at half pay in order to pursue a well-defined research project. Among individual research grants, one of the most notable was the $134,000 received in 1982 by Prof. Christopher Chetsanga (biology) from the National Cancer Institute. Prof. Chetsanga's research results on the deterioration and restoration of cells attracted international attention. In July 1983, Prof. Leslie Tentler (history) was commissioned by the Catholic Archdiocese of Detroit to write a history of the Archdiocese, and was given a three-year research appointment (1983-1986) to complete the task. Prof. Richard Axsom (art history) gained national recognition in the fall of 1982 as the curator of an exhibit of the prints of Frank Stella, which opened in Ann Arbor and then traveled to major museums in the United States. In November 1984, Prof. John Kotre (psychology) was awarded a grant of $2,150,000 from the Annenberg Foundation and the Corporation for Public Broadcasting to produce a series of public television and radio programs on "The Psychological Seasons of Human Life." Prof. Tsung-Yen Na (mechanical engineering), on the basis of his scholarly achievements, was appointed in the fall of 1984 to a five-year term as the second William Stirton Professor at UM-D (Peter Amann was the first). Another named chair was funded by the accounting firm of Ernst and Whinney for an initial five-year period, beginning in 1985. Dr. William Culp, professor of accounting, was approved in December 1984 as the first holder of this chair.

Other Developments

Student Activities. There were several significant developments relating to students between 1980 and 1984. Student minority enrollment reached a record 9.6 percent of total enrollment in the fall of 1983, attesting to the plurality of cultures served by UM-D. The academic level of entering students remained high, with average ACT scores of 23 and average GPA's of 3.3. Student activities were on the rise in the early '80's. "Spirit Week," a student-originated and sponsored event in 1982, sought to bring in people from the community to see the campus in operation and to be hosted and entertained by both students and faculty. The event was repeated in 1983, and the third Spirit Week was held in October 1984 as a part of the 25th Anniversary celebration. UM-D's ice hockey team did its part to bring people to campus in 1981-82 by its distinguished season of 23 wins, six losses, and one tie. It has gone on to the NAIA tournament for four successive years, never finishing lower than fourth. One student activity of long standing was lost during this period, however; the "Hinge," an on-campus coffee house which was set in the basement of Fair Lane from 1967-77 and in ROC from 1978 to 1980, finally closed down in the spring of 1980. Nevertheless, the University Mall has been the setting for frequent concerts and performances by outside groups since it was opened in 1979.

Retirements, Deaths, and Resignations. Because many UM-D faculty and staff have reached either the time for retirement or a point of mobility in their careers, an unprecedented number of them have left the campus in the last four or five years. Herschel Wallace, the original director of student affairs at the Dearborn Center, and Frances Cousens, professor of sociology, both retired in December 1979. Prof Alburey Castell, who came in 1974 (when he was already two years past retirement) as a visiting professor of philosophy, left UM-D in the summer of 1981, having stamped on many memories his dogged insistence on "the second sense of 'rationality'" and his equally dogged and personal resistance to the ideas of B. F. Skinner. Thomas Schroth, the stern-visaged but hardworking coordinator for engineering co-op students since 1962, retired in December 1981. Emmanuel Hertzler ("Hertz" to all of his colleagues), the original biologist at UM-D and a tireless innovator in curriculum, retired in February 1982. Burton Harrison's retirement in July 1983 has already been noted.

Many on the campus mourned the death of John Dempsey, former chairman of the LSA Division, on April 2, 1982. In May 1982, Soon Park Chung, associate professor of mathematics, was killed in an automobile accident, and her department was sadly reminded of the violent death of another one of their faculty, Carl Rasmussen, who was shot to death in August of 1979. Dr. William Stirton, the founding chief executive officer of UM-D, died in March 1983. On March 31, 1983, a stained glass sculpture, hung across from the first floor stairs in the Library, commemorated the death in March 1979 of Diane Culp, a campus librarian and the wife of Prof. William Culp (accounting).

A number of faculty and staff members have left UM-D—or have taken leaves of absence in anticipation of leaving—in just the past year (through September 1984): William Agresti (industrial and systems engineering), associate dean of the School of Engineering; John Potts in physics; Christopher Chetsanga in biology; Denis Dutton (philosophy), founder and editor of the journal *Philosophy and Literature;* Sal Rinella, vice-chancellor for business and finance; C. Edward Wall, director of the library; and Barbara Forisha-Kovach (psychology), former chairperson of the Department of Behavioral Sciences.

A great deal of UM-D's strength has been its ability to attract first-rate faculty, but a consequence of that accomplishment is that such faculty members also have opportunities for challenging work elsewhere; indeed, it may be taken as a mark of the quality of the institution's personnel that they are invited to accept appointments elsewhere, either temporarily or permanently. It is therefore with mixed emotions that the UM-D community sees members of its faculty and staff moving on to other positions: such moves certainly entail the loss of people who have proved themselves valuable colleagues, but their efforts have established a firmer ground on which to recruit their replacements. The challenge is to maintain former standards of hiring and to present the potential of the campus in a positive way at a time when the pains of consolidation are still fresh.

Protecting a Gift
Orin Gelderloos, professor of biological
science, in the Natural Area, a 70-acre
nature preserve which was a part of the
original Henry Ford estate.
Philip T. Dattilo

7
Concluding
Remarks

Most people who have been associated with The University of Michigan-Dearborn for more than five years will likely feel that this history of the campus leaves out something vital to them; and they're probably right. Any enterprise as complex as a University campus cannot be viewed completely by one person even for a limited period of time, let alone for an expanse of over 25 years. What you have just read, then, is necessarily based on the limited perspective of an individual faculty member who has added to his personal knowledge of 19 years at UM-D a rather-too-hasty survey of newspaper clippings, University newsletters, administrative records, and personal interviews. Nevertheless, my several months of absorption in this material has inevitably either produced or confirmed some opinions about the character of the campus, about how and why it has arrived where it is, and about the strongest points on which it can build for the next 25 or 50 years.

Before I list these opinions, however, perhaps it would be helpful for me to comment on how the particular circumstances at UM-D have affected my own professional career, and how the pattern of my experience reflects something about the history of UM-D. I came to the campus in 1965, when the little band of faculty and staff was finding it increasingly difficult to defend its comfortable but obscure existence. Since this was my first faculty appointment, I was barely aware of the campus's overall problems before I was plunged, along with everybody else, into what seemed the only solution to those problems—rapid, radical expansion. Because this development meant that even the inexperienced faculty got pressed into very responsible kinds of service, I was drafted, as were others my age, into making decisions on curriculum, hiring, administrative structure and policy, and other important matters which at other schools might have been out of my sphere of influence until I was old enough to write the history of the campus. In many ways, I have matured

Top left: The Fair Lane mansion viewed from the Rouge River. Top right: Peggy Campbell, volunteer chair of the Fair Lane Development Committee, in the foyer of the Fair Lane mansion. Bottom left: Swatantra Kachhal, associate professor of industrial and systems engineering, recipient of Distinguished Tenured Faculty Award of 1977-78. Bottom right: Carolyn Kraus, lecturer in English composition, recipient of Distinguished Non-Tenured Faculty Award of 1979-80. *All Philip T. Dattilo*

Concluding Remarks

with UM-D, coming while the idyllic atmosphere of its infancy was still upon it, then living through its adolescent and early adult growing pains, and now being ensconced on a campus so changed and expanded that its condition in 1965 seems sometimes a very distant memory. My position constitutes something of a paradox, since I am an "old timer" who still has a fair number of years before retirement. That I am not alone in being a relatively young senior faculty member is an indication of what is distinctive about UM-D.

The core of my observations concerning the history of this institution, then, lies in its particular mix of sometimes contradictory elements; youth and experience; traditional academic quality coupled with experimental and practical programs; being part of a sophisticated major University but located in a mostly conservative, middle-class suburb; and protecting a 70-acre nature preserve in the middle of an industrial metropolitan area. All of these couplings have created tensions and problems, but they have also given UM-D its chief strengths, and they are the springboard for my final observations about the past development and the present potentialities of the campus.

1) UM-D has produced some of its best results when it has taken good ideas which were being too narrowly pursued and has broadened their application (e.g., off-campus educational experience, interaction with business and industry).

2) The standard of good teaching at UM-D was established by the early resident faculty, and that ideal has been perpetuated in the hiring of faculty ever since. Teaching quality and the intellectual vitality that goes with it have been the bedrock of UM-D's reputation as a *bona fide* unit of The University of Michigan.

3) The absence of extensive graduate programs at UM-D, coupled with the pressure for faculty research which comes from being a part of The University of Michigan, has brought about a closer relationship between faculty scholarship and undergraduate teaching than is usually the case. However, although this fusion of scholarly activity and undergraduate education has been the backbone of the campus's academic strength and reputation, it has also been a source of significant frustration to faculty, who are sometimes hard pressed to fulfill the demands of both conscientious teaching and productive research, to say nothing of the heavy service load that they have shouldered as part of a developing campus.

4) Although the original Ford gift of the campus to The University of Michigan did not produce what either of them hoped for, and although neither of them followed through sufficiently in support of the campus in the early years, their original determination to maintain in the institu-

tion both high academic quality and a practical tie with the business and industrial community somehow evoked in the faculty a similar commitment that proved to be effective, even though it often fomented conflict. This aspect of the campus's legacy has been a vital part of its strength, although its renewal over the years has involved a number of stages of metamorphosis.

5) While both the liberal arts faculty and the faculty of the professional units (Engineering and Management) each tend to think that the other group poses a threat to the appropriate focus of the campus, neither could exist at UM-D without the other. The expansion in the seventies had to take place primarily in the liberal arts; but if the professional schools had not been there in the first place, there would have been nothing to expand.

6) The natural and historical attractions of the Fair Lane Estate have been an indispensable element in creating and maintaining public concern about the fortunes of UM-D. The voices among both the faculty and the public which have defended the Natural Area and the mansion from abuse or neglect have often been lonely ones, and the UM-D administration has not always dealt wisely in these matters; but the present constructive use of these resources and the increasing realization of their value is a tribute to such people as biologists Emmanuel Hertzler, Calvin DeWitt, and Orin Gelderloos and community leader Iris Becker.

And what are the implications of these observations for the present state of UM-D? In the first place, the institution is playing to its historical strengths when it maintains that its chief contribution to the communities of Metropolitan Detroit is providing an integrated selection of both professional and liberal arts disciplines of a quality commensurate with being a unit of The University of Michigan. That means accepting and blending a certain diversity of focuses, expertise, specific objectives, academic methods, and students; that is what the builders of UM-D have done, whether on purpose or by accident; but if it continues it will not be by accident.

Secondly, UM-D would apparently do well to cultivate its community ties as effectively as possible, as indeed it has begun to do in its more recent years; it is these relationships that will determine the long-term success or failure of the campus.

Thirdly, in the midst of increasing competition for matriculants in higher education, UM-D has by the pattern of its development produced a distinctive set of advantages to offer students: relative smallness with the University of Michigan name; intellectually stimulating instructors who take time to talk to students; and a mixture and variety of programs—both traditional and innovative,

Finally, UM-D should continue to remember the value of the original Ford gift to the University—not only the academic buildings and the ground on which they stand, but also the woods, the mansion, and its grounds. These, as well as the more conventional educational resources of the campus, are trusts held for the community, and they stand as unique natural and historical laboratories within The University of Michigan. And since gifts are never fully enjoyed unless they are put to use responsibly, this campus and its resources—natural, human, and financial—must continue to be renewed by the University's active search for the best way to put people in touch with these resources.

Perhaps, since the world and its institutions are mutable, the 25-year experiment that The University of Michigan-Dearborn embodies will not be around in 2009 to celebrate a golden anniversary; but if that is the case, it will not be because there has been any shortage of examples in its first quarter of a century of either mistakes to be avoided or successes to be encouraged by. If the institution is still functioning successfully in its golden year, it is to be hoped that it will have used and renewed its resources in the second 25 years in a notable way; but UM-D could be happy indeed, at the end of its second quarter of a century, to have accomplished as much in relation to its resources, either by design or by chance, as it did from 1959 through 1984.

Appendix
One

A List of Principal
and Key Documents Relating
to the History of UM-D

Note: These documents are available in the supplementary volume, Important Documents in the History of UM-Dearborn, and/or in the UM-D Library Archives, unless otherwise noted. Documents marked with an asterisk (*) are reproduced as a whole or in part in Appendix Two.

1. General Sources:

    A. UM-D Library Archives

        1) Newspaper clippings and public relations materials, filed by years, 1959-1984.

        2) Student newspapers: *The Fairlane* (January-May 1962); the *Dearborn Wolverine* (November 1963-January 1964); *Ad Hoc* (December 1964-May 1967, October 1969-May 1970); *Michigan Journal* (September 1970-present).

        3) University Relations staff newsletters; *Gildow Gazette* (July-December 1968); *Dearborn Campus Bulletin* (fall 1970-summer 1973); *Reporter* (fall 1973-present.)

        4) Chancellor's annual report and occasional "From the Chancellor's Desk" memos to campus community (late 1972 to present).

        5) Annual report of chief academic officer (E. Arden, 1972 to present).

    B. Bentley Historical Library (Ann Arbor, North Campus).

        1) Files of former UM President Harlan Hatcher, Boxes 16, 27, 31, and 37.

        2) Files of Marvin Niehuss and Harold Dorr.

        3) Clippings File, Box 9.

        4) Taped interviews by Sharon Campbell with UM-D and UM-AA personnel, 1972.

2. Minutes of initial meetings between Ford Motor Co. and U. of M. officials on establishment of University branch in Dearborn (January-April, 1956).

3. U. of M. proposal (June 1956) for specifications of UM-Dearborn Center.

*4. Letters from President Hatcher to Henry Ford II (November 5, 1956) requesting site and capital funds for UM-Dearborn Center.

*5. News release on announcement of Ford gift to found UM-Dearborn Center (December 17, 1956).

6. Letter from Harold Dorr to Charles Odegaard on 12 points of agreement between Ford Motor Co. and the U. of M. on Dearborn Center (January 7, 1957).

* 6a. Minutes of U. of M. Conference of Deans (January 9, 1957).

* 7. Legislative Resolution expressing appreciation to Ford Motor Co. for gift and urging U. of M. to accept it (January 9-10, 1957).

* 8. Section of Regents' Minutes accepting Ford gift (February 1957).

9. Report of the Walker (LSA) Committee on academic program and structure for the Dearborn Center (June 13, 1957).

*10. Report of the "Committee on the Organization of the Dearborn Center," chaired by H. Dorr (November 19, 1957); Regents' Communication, December 31, 1957).

*11. Section of Regents' Minutes approving bylaws which authorized and set the structure of the Dearborn Center (January 10, 1958); Regents' Bylaws, 1958, Chapter XXXIII.

12. Statement by U. of M. President Harlan Hatcher at beginning of construction of Dearborn Center (May 22, 1958).

13. Interview with William Stirton on the Dearborn Center *(Michigan Alumnus*, March 14, 1959).

14. Article by William Stirton on the Dearborn Center in *Ford Times,* February 1960.

15. Memo from R. Lee Brummet on first term of UM-DC business administration program (February 16, 1960).

16. Notes from William Stirton to UM-DC faculty on the Center (summer 1960).

17. Article by William Stirton on Dearborn Campus in a book, *Experimental Colleges* (1964).

18. Letter from John Dempsey (Chairman, UM-D LSA Div.) to Vice-President Allan Smith on state of Dearborn Campus (December 2, 1965). [CASL Administration Files]

19. Letter to Harlan Hatcher from William Stirton on problems of Dearborn Campus (May 2, 1966).

20. Ad in *Time* magazine on Dearborn Campus cooperative education opportunities in all divisions (July 5, 1968).

21. Charge to Dearborn Campus Planning Study Committee (November 27, 1968).

*22. Report of the Dearborn Campus Planning Study Committee (May 1969).

*23. Section of Regents' Minutes on response to special reports on UM-D and UM-Flint (November 1969).

24. Report of Dearborn Campus Freshman/Sophomore Curriculum Committee (Spring 1970).

25. Special issue of the *University Record* on UM-Dearborn (October 25, 1971).

26. Chancellor Leonard Goodall's Inaugural Address (January 23, 1972).

27. Chancellor Goodall's State of the Campus address for 1971-72 (October 4, 1972).

28. "From the Chancellor's Desk" on UM-D long range planning and goals (December 15, 1972).

29. UM-D Self-Study Report for the North Central Association (January 1974).

*29a. UM-D Bylaws (March 1973).

*30. Regents' Minutes approving new UM-D structure (May 1973).

31. UM-D Long Range Development Plan—Summary Report (July 20, 1973).

32. Memo from Chancellor Goodall describing land exchange with Ford Motor Land Development Co. and Wayne County Road Commission (July 30, 1974).

33. News Release on Goals Statement for UM-D approved by Regents (September 20, 1974).

34. Chancellor Goodall's Annual Report for 1975-76 (5-year overview)—November 1976.

35. Memo from Task Force on Faculty Concerns (April 15, 1977).

36. UM-D Role and Mission Statement, drafted by Long Range Planning Committee (April 1979).

36a. UM-D Mission and Purposes Statement for UM-D, July 1983.

37. UM-D Self-Study Report for North Central Association (January 1984).

Appendix Two

Copies of Selected Key Documents

Appendix 2.1a: Letter from Harlan Hatcher to Henry Ford II

University of Michigan, Ann Arbor, Office of the President
November 5, 1956

Mr. Henry Ford II, President
Ford Motor Company
American Road
Dearborn, Michigan

Dear Mr. Ford:

The University of Michigan has been earnestly considering ways and means of meeting the need for more college-trained graduates in specialized fields. We believe that an effective way of doing this would be to extend our program to a select area outside of Ann Arbor. Specifically, the University of Michigan proposes the establishment of a University Center in Dearborn which would offer the last two years' work leading to the Bachelor's degree in Engineering, Business Administration, and in Literature, Science, and the Arts, as well as the Master's degree in certain selected fields of Engineering and Business Administration. The Engineering and Business Administration courses would be on a cooperative basis, with the students alternating periods of instruction with periods of work experience.

The University of Michigan invites the Ford Motor Company to participate in the development of this proposed educational center by conveying to the University approximately 200 acres of land now owned by the Company in the City of Dearborn. Among locations of this size, the Fair Lane property and undeveloped land adjacent thereto would be by far the most satisfactory from all standpoints, including accessibility, central location, historical significance, and attractiveness of physical surroundings. A formal and specific request that these properties be granted and conveyed to the University, under specified conditions, accompanies this letter.

We ask your thoughtful consideration of our request.

Sincerely yours,
Harlan Hatcher

Appendix 2.1b: Site Request

A shortage of college-trained manpower to supply the needs of the increasingly complex technology and organization of an expanding economy is today a major national problem. In some fields, such as engineering and science, this shortage is already so acute that it may threaten loss of the technological and economic lead which we now hold over the rest of the world. Certainly it threatens to slow the technological and productive progress upon which our continued domestic prosperity depends.

This acute need for an increase in college graduates with specialized training comes at a time when the colleges and universities of the nation are short of facilities to accommodate properly even the students they now have. Vastly larger numbers of young people are already in the elementary and high schools and will soon be pressing for admission to college. To provide for these additional students, the colleges and universities of the nation will need to increase their physical plant and other facilities by at least fifty percent within the next five to ten years. This is a task of enormous proportions, and its accomplishment will require not only the most imaginative and ingenious planning by educators, but also the most understanding and generous financial support on the part of state legislatures, educational and charitable foundations, and other contributors.

For some years, the University of Michigan has been aware of and planning for this impending emergency in higher education in Michigan. It has been engaged for some time in exploring ways and means by which it might meet most effectively its responsibilities in providing the enlarged educational opportunities which are demanded by the State's growing population and expanding economy. To this end the University has developed a planned program of expansion in keeping with its history and responsibility to the State which it believes will make most effective use of its unique and special educational resources. This program has the following major components:

A. Vigorous expansion on the Ann Arbor campus of facilities for those things which can best be done there. An example of this type of expansion is the development of the North Campus for research, advanced engineering and certain other professional programs.

B. Extension of the University's facilities to other communities in the State where clear needs exist and where such communities are prepared to assist the State by contributing toward the cost of new facilities. This part of the program has been initiated by the establishment of the Flint College of the University of Michigan where the community supplied the physical facilities, and the operation of the college will be in close co-operation with the existing junior college.

C. Exploration of the potentialities for development of co-operative programs between the University and employers in those professional fields which lend themselves to this type of program. In such programs the students would alternate periods of instruction with periods of practical experience and training on the job.

The co-operative program, which brings together in a mutual effort the experience and resources of educational institutions and of employers, offers a promising means of attack upon the current shortage of trained manpower. Because of the practical and realistic work experience provided in co-operative education, students are able to put their academic training to productive use sooner than would be the case in a conventional program. Co-operative programs also tend to increase the numbers of young people seeking specialized training, because the employment feature of the program opens the opportunity of college education to students who would otherwise be unable to afford it.

The University of Michigan has not yet initiated a major program in the co-operative area, but is desirous of doing so. As a result of exploratory studies carried on over a considerable period, the University believes that the Wayne County area offers an exceptionally favorable opportunity for the development of a university center with major emphasis upon co-operative programs in the fields of engineering and business administration. Dearborn in particular is at the center of an area with a large and growing population, including large numbers of people whose jobs call for college and technical training. The co-operative pattern, at the lower college levels, has already been successfully and extensively developed by the Henry Ford Community College of Dearborn.

The University proposes the establishment of a University Center in Dearborn which would offer the last two years' work leading to the Bachelor's degree in Engineering, Business Administration and Literature, Science, and the Arts, as well as the Master's degree in certain selected fields of Engineering and Business Administration. The Engineering and Business Administration courses would be on a co-operative basis, with the students alternating periods of instruction with periods of work experience.

While the proposed Center would be an independent unit of the University of Michigan, it would function in close co-operation with the Henry Ford Community College to provide, for students of the area, an opportunity for four years of college work while living at home. This is a pattern which is now working successfully in Flint.

Another feature of the proposed Center would be a substantial offering of late afternoon and evening classes in order that persons employed full time might have opportunities to pursue courses leading to advanced degrees in engineering, business administration and related fields.

Careful studies have been made of the proposed curricula and the space and facilities needed for a unit of sufficient size to permit economical operation of the type of instruction planned. The scope of the program is set out in the statement attached to this request.

It is estimated that a minimum of $6,500,000 will be needed for buildings and equipment to initiate such a Center, exclusive of land cost. The Ford Motor Company Fund, in response to our request, has made a pledge of a grant in this amount for the construction and equipment of the facilities, contingent upon: (a) the obtaining of a satisfactory site in the Dearborn area, and (b) the approval of the plan by the Legislature of the State of Michigan.

A satisfactory site for the proposed Center, allowing for future expansion would require a minimum of 200 acres. Among locations of this size in the area, the Fair Lane property and undeveloped land adjacent thereto owned by Ford Motor Company would be by far the most satisfactory from all standpoints, including accessibility, central location, historical significance, and attractiveness of physical surroundings.

The University requests, therefore, that the Ford Motor Company grant and convey to the Regents of the University of Michigan for educational purposes a minimum of 200 acres of land, including Fair Lane and adjacent properties, for the proposed University of Michigan-Dearborn Center. The actual transfer of the land, if offered, would be contingent upon approval of the plan by the Legislature of the State of Michigan.

If this land, as well as the pledged funds for the construction of physical facilities, can be assured promptly, the University will proceed at once to obtain legislative approval of the project and will expect to begin classes in the new Center not later than the fall of 1959. In the meantime the University will seek to enlist a maximum number of employers in co-operating with and contributing to the undertaking.

We feel that the proposed Center can make an important pioneering contribution to the solution of a major national problem of unusual local significance. We ask your thoughtful consideration of our request.

Appendix 2.2: News Release on Gift from Ford

From the University of Michigan News Service
3564 Administration Bldg., Ann Arbor
Telephone NOrmandy 3-1511, Ext. 2623

December 17, 1956

Gifts of 210 acres and $6,500,000 have been offered to the University of Michigan by Ford Motor Company and the Ford Motor Company Fund for establishment of a Dearborn Center of the university with an enrollment of more than 2,700 students.

Dr. Harlan Hatcher, president of the university, announced today that the school's regents have accepted the offers tentatively.

Dr. Hatcher said the university had proposed the new center after studying means for meeting the need for more college-trained graduates in specialized fields. These studies indicated Dearborn as a logical location for the center and, as a result, Ford Motor Company was invited to participate in its establishment, he said.

The land offered to the university by Ford Motor Company includes Fair Lane, former estate of Henry Ford and present home of the Ford Archives. The $6,500,000 offered by the Ford Motor Company Fund would provide buildings for the proposed center.

Plans for the Dearborn Center were announced at Fair Lane at a joint conference of university officials headed by President Hatcher and Ford Motor Company officials headed by Henry Ford II, president and Ernest R. Breech, chairman of the board.

President Hatcher said the offers of land and money had been accepted by the regents contingent on the state's willingness to provide funds to operate the proposed center.

He added that the combined gifts are the largest ever made by a company and its charitable fund to an educational institution, and that they would do much to help meet "an impending emergency in higher education in Michigan."

Commenting on the "far-sighted proposal" of the University of Michigan to establish the center, Henry Ford II said it offers Ford Motor Company a means for "expressing positively our belief in industry's responsibility to education."

"Ford Motor Company feels fortunate in being able to join in this practical attack on the problem of a more adequate system of higher education," he said. "We confidently expect that other private sources will join forces in making this new college one of the finest educational centers in the land…"

Mr. Ford also stated that he believed a precedent was being established by which "other American companies may contribute materially to meeting one of our nation's most urgent problems, while leaving the actual educating job where it should be—in the hands of our professional educators."

The University of Michigan-Dearborn Center would be an integral part of the university, cooperating closely with Dearborn's Henry Ford Community College to provide the area with a four-year college. The University of Michigan and the Flint Junior College now offer a four-year program in Flint.

President Hatcher said that if adequate appropriations are approved by the state legislature, the Dearborn Center will be open no later than 1959 and possibly by the fall of 1958.

He said the Dearborn Center, located in the heart of a highly diversified industrial area, would provide the university with its first major opportunity to develop cooperative education—combining classroom and shop instruction with practical work in industry. Students in engineering and business administration at the junior, senior and graduate levels would participate in the program, he added.

In addition to engineering and business administration courses, the Dearborn Center would offer junior and senior programs in liberal arts and sciences, as well as late-afternoon and evening instruction leading to advanced degrees in engineering, business administration and related fields…

University officials estimate the following enrollment within three years after the Dearborn Center reaches full operation:

	Type of Experience		
Unit	Study	Work	Total
Undergraduate Engineering	512	512	1024
Graduate Engineering	182	182	364
Undergraduate Business Adm.	248	248	496
Graduate Business Adm.	143	143	286
Literature, Science, and the Arts	600		600
	1685	1085	2770

12/56

Appendix 2.3: Conference of Deans on Establishment of Dearborn Center

FROM MINUTES OF THE CONFERENCE OF DEANS
The University of Michigan

January 9, 1957

Dr. Hatcher said that the negotiations concerning the gift to the University from the Ford Motor Company, announced December 17, had to be carried out with extraordinary delicacy. The gift of the Dearborn Center by the Ford Motor Company was accepted by the University for pretty much the same reasons it had for accepting the gift from the Mott Foundation— as an answer to the increase in student population in the State of Michigan, and particularly at the University of Michigan in Ann Arbor. He said in moving to Dearborn we followed the principle of accepting invitations from communities geographically correctly located that offer fine support for higher education. "Both at Flint and at Dearborn there are good junior colleges that provide sound preparation for the upper two years of university work," he said. In addition to the strong community base found at Flint and at Dearborn, both have provided money and land. Dr. Hatcher added that the Legislature will have sufficient time to plan its financial support for the University's Dearborn Center.

Dean Dorr referred to the public announcement made jointly on December 17 by the Ford Motor Company and the University of Michigan of the gift to the University of $6,500,000 and 210 acres of land at Fair Lane. The Dean said that approximately a year ago President Hatcher had detected some desire on the part of the Ford Motor Company to support higher education in the State of Michigan through the University of Michigan; that Mr. Bugas, on the part of the Ford Motor Company, and Mr. Niehuss, on the part of the University, and later he himself had been charged with continuing an examination of possible negotiations; that Deans Brown and Stevenson were also brought in for discussion at an early date, since the work at the Dearborn Center will emphasize mechanical and industrial engineering and business administration.

Plans from the outset, the Dean continued, highlighted a cooperative plan of academic study plus work in industry. Supplementary courses in liberal arts also were in the plan. The Dean said it was assumed from the beginning that such courses would be provided, although no commitments had yet been made covering the nature and scope of the work in liberal arts and sciences. The discussions have constantly focused around the extent to which such a program would benefit the entire Dearborn community. Necessary library and laboratory facilities will be needed to offer upper-class courses in the humanities, mathematics, sciences, and social sciences. The work to be offered will be limited to third- and fourth-year under-graduate courses and first-year courses on the graduate level.

Two hundred and fifteen thousand square feet of building space will be needed for class-room accommodations, Dean Dorr said. No part of the Ford Motor Company gift has been earmarked by the Company for particular purposes; the University is quite free to develop an educational program without being hampered in its plans by any limiting definitions in the gift.

Dean Dorr read from a letter he had addressed under date of January 7, 1957, to Deans Brown, Odegaard, and Stevenson. In the letter he emphasized that the University is committed to attempt the following:

"(1) to provide, within the limits of the gift, facilities—including laboratories and libraries for the numbers of students mentioned in the course of the discussions;

"(2) to attempt to provide cooperative study-work opportunities for undergraduates—and probably graduates—in Mechanical and Industrial Engineering and Business Administration.

"(3) to offer only the junior and senior years of work and one year of graduate work in Engineering and Business Administration;

"(4) to work cooperatively with the Henry Ford Community College to provide four years of college work in the Dearborn community;

"(5) to provide an instructional staff which is *not* inferior to our campus faculties;

"(6) to offer programs of study which are *not* inferior in quality to, although they may be somewhat different from, those offered on the campus at Ann Arbor;

"(7) to confer degrees parallel to those conferred for comparable work completed on campus;

"(8) to provide at least a minimum of student service facilities;

"(9) to consider the 'quarter' rather than the 'semester' plan;

"(10) to offer a complete program of studies in Engineering and Business Administration in each of the four quarters;

"(11) to consult with industry in the planning and administration of the cooperative programs;

"(12) to secure adequate operating funds."

Dean Dorr elaborated on the point made earlier that the program would be one of academic study and work in industry. Dean Dorr believes "that the quarter system can be more readily accommodated to a sound cooperative study-work program than can the semester plan." In the plans which have been made to date concerning the program at the Dearborn Center, it is assumed that all units that participate in the Center will use a common academic calendar.

The Dean said that discussions were proceeding on other problems, such as internal organization and over-all administration; the relationship of the Center to the Dearborn community, with special reference to the Henry Ford Community College; policy questions, including administrative relationships with comparable campus units; educational standards; staff recruitment; etc.

Vice-President Stirton, who has been intimately connected with the plans for the establishment of the Dearborn Center and who is charged with communicating the budgetary needs of the Center to the Legislature, said that the general community acceptance and understanding of the plan were most gratifying; that this Center is not a handmaiden of the Ford Motor Company; that other motor companies in the area will cooperate in the work-study program; that this gift is not one of tax convenience to the Ford Motor Company.

Vice-President Pierpont added that Professor Dorr had accepted the chairmanship of the continuing Planning Committee for the Dearborn Center.

Appendix 2.4a: Legislative Resolution on Ford Gift

The University of Michigan Board of Regents Minutes, January Meeting, 1957

The Regents acknowledged the following Senate Concurrent Resolution No. 5, adopted by the Senate January 9, 1957, and by the House January 10, 1957:

A CONCURRENT RESOLUTION COMMENDING THE FORD MOTOR COMPANY AND ITS ASSOCIATED FUND FOR THEIR GIFT OF LANDS AND MONEY TO THE UNIVERSITY OF MICHIGAN AND URGING ITS ACCEPTANCE BY THE REGENTS OF THE UNIVERSITY OF MICHIGAN.

WHEREAS, The state of Michigan is acutely sensitive to the mounting crisis in American education involving large capital expenditures; and

WHEREAS, Assuring opportunity to deserving boys and girls for education beyond the high school level will require an expansion in the next decade of over 50 per cent of the physical plants and facilities of our universities and colleges; and

WHEREAS, Providing for these needs requires concerted action by educators, private industry, and other private groups, as well as by the state legislatures and the federal government; and

WHEREAS, It is imperative that we examine and undertake various educational patterns in determining the total solution to our educational needs; and

WHEREAS, The co-operative program which brings together in a mutual effort the experience and resources of educational institutions and of employers offers one promising means of attack upon the current shortage of trained manpower; and

WHEREAS, Gifts of 210 acres of land including Fair Lane, the former estate of Henry Ford, and $6,500,000.00 have been offered to the University of Michigan by the Ford Motor Company and the Ford Motor Company Fund for the establishment of a Dearborn Center of the University; and

WHEREAS, These facilities and funds would make a real and significant contribution to the solution of the needs of higher education in the state of Michigan; and

WHEREAS, The splendid example set by the Ford Motor Company and the Ford Motor Company Fund should stimulate and encourage the awarding of other gifts and grants from industries and organizations which will aid the state of Michigan in its total educational needs; now therefore be it

Resolved by the Senate (the House of Representatives concurring), That the Michigan legislature warmly commends the Ford Motor Company and its associated Fund for the generous gift to the University of Michigan; for its alertness, in recognizing the vital educational needs of the state of Michigan; and for its courage in setting an example which other industries may emulate; and be it further

Resolved, That this body urges The Regents of the University of Michigan to accept this generous gift and thus encourage private industry and other private groups to contribute materially to our state's and nation's urgent needs, while leaving the actual educating responsibility where it should be—in the hands of our professional educators.

Appendix 2.4b: Regents' Acceptance of Ford Gift

The President presented a letter from C. J. Fellrath, Secretary of the Ford Motor Company, offering to the University "Fair Lane," the former residence of Mr. and Mrs. Henry Ford, and 210 acres of land immediately surrounding it. He also read a letter from Allen W. Merrell, Vice-President of the Ford Motor Company Fund, offering the University $6,500,000 to establish the Dearborn Center.

Ford Motor Company: Gifts from

In view of the legislative approval expressed unanimously by the joint Senate-House resolutions of January 9, 1957, the Regents consider the conditions to have been met and gratefully accept the gifts offered by the Ford Motor Company and the Ford Motor Company Fund.

Appendix 2.5a: Communication to Regents from Harold Dorr

UNIVERSITY OF MICHIGAN
ANN ARBOR

To the Honorable Board of Regents:

Your attention is invited to the following, for consideration if possible at your meeting called for January 10, 1958.

DEARBORN CENTER
ADMINISTRATIVE ORGANIZATION

I have been instructed to present on behalf of the committee named below a proposal for the administrative organization of the Dearborn Center, and to recommend its adoption.

Because of the pioneering character of the venture, the spread of the educational program, the place of the Center in the Dearborn community, the proposed relationships with industry and business and, to the University, the unique purposes and objectives of the Center, the administrative organization of the Center, and its place in the structure of the University have been carefully studied. Exploratory discussions have been carried on over a period of several months. The proposals which have been advanced for the organization of the Center range from complete dependence upon or incorporation into existing departments on the Ann Arbor campus, to the creation of a separate unit possessing those qualities of autonomy which characterize the existing Schools and Colleges. Even though these diverse points of view were ably supported, discussions appeared to reveal a consensus favoring a middle position.

These discussions were formalized when, under date of October 31, 1957, Vice President Niehuss requested Deans Attwood, Dorr, Odegaard, Sawyer, and Stevenson to serve as a Committee on Organization for the Dearborn Center. The committee re-evaluated the earlier proposals but quickly shifted its attention from the extremes to a middle ground position. In the opinion of the committee, it would be unwise to establish the Dearborn Center, originally, either as a completely separate unit of the University or as a simple extension of existing Schools and Colleges.

The committee believes that the Dearborn Center should be granted a degree of independence which will encourage it to develop an academic personality in its own right, to become identified with the Dearborn community, to respond to the educational needs of that community, and to accommodate itself readily to the educational problems inherent in the purposes and objectives of the venture. The Dearborn Center, therefore, should be free to experiment with problems of curriculum, instructional methods and external relationships.

The committee believes that the Center, especially in the formative years, should have the opportunity to share the stability, the strength and the experiences of the established Schools and Colleges, that it should be responsive to guidance and direction from the older units, but that it should not be subjected to their direct control.

The committee believes that its proposal balances these competing factors to the advantage of the Dearborn Center and advances an organization plan which is administratively sound. The committee believes, also, that the proposal possesses elements of flexibility which will permit orderly development either in the direction of greater autonomy or of gradual departmental integration—whichever direction experience dictates.

A summary of recommendations and a copy of the proposal accompany this communication.

Date _____ December 31, _____ 19 57 _____

Signed _____ [Harold M Dorr] _____

Appendix 2.5b: Recommendations of Dorr Committee

DEARBORN CENTER
SUMMARY OF RECOMMENDATIONS

1) That the proposed educational unit be officially designated "The Dearborn Center of the University of Michigan."
2) That programs of study be limited to the junior and senior years and to the first year of graduate studies.
3) That the University acknowledge an intent to provide a program of "Cooperative Education," alternating equal periods of campus study and job experiences.
4) That the Dearborn Center be organized originally in three Divisions: Business Administration, Engineering, and the Liberal Arts and Sciences.
5) That eventually the faculties of the several Divisions of the Dearborn Center assume the same responsibilities and perform the same functions as are vested in the governing faculties of the established schools and colleges of the University.
6) That until such time as the faculties are properly organized to assume their responsibilities and functions, these responsibilities and functions be vested in three standing committees—one to be created for each Division.
7) That the executive functions of the Dearborn Center be performed by a Dean and an Executive Committee.
8) That the Dean of the Dearborn Center be vested with the authority, functions and responsibilities vested in deans of academic units by the Bylaws of the Board of Regents and the conventions of the University, and empowered to perform such other duties as may be assigned from time to time.
9) That the Horace H. Rackham School of Graduate Studies or, in appropriate cases, another unit of the University, be authorized to offer one year of graduate studies through any Division of the Dearborn Center.

The language used in the statement of "purpose" and "organization" and in the definition of functions and responsibilities, follows as closely as possible the text of comparable passages in the By-Laws. It is assumed that "governing faculties," "Dean," "Executive Committee," and "department" used in the proposal will be understood as defined and used elsewhere in the By-Laws. On the other hand, "Division" as here used is to be distinguished from those divisions of the University established in Chapter XXVI.

The text of the recommendation is presented with the understanding that, if approved, chapter and sections will be renumbered to conform to the text of the By-Laws.

Appendix 2.6: Bylaws Establishing the Dearborn Center

from University of Michigan Regents Bylaws, 1958

CHAPTER XXXIII. DEARBORN CENTER

Sec. 33.01. General Purpose. The Dearborn Center shall be maintained for the purpose of providing instruction and conducting research at upper class and graduate levels, in business administration, engineering, and the liberal arts and sciences, and in such other fields of knowledge as may be designated from time to time by the Board of Regents. In business administration, engineering, and to such extent as shall be deemed advisable, in the liberal arts and sciences, the Center shall provide in conjunction with business, industry, and public or semi-public agencies a cooperative educational program. The work-experience assignments shall be an integral part of the total educational program, and shall be planned and administered to afford maximum learning opportunities and to ensure a substantial educational contribution in each of the designated areas.

Sec. 33.02. Organization. The Center shall be organized originally in three Divisions: Business Administration, Engineering, and the Liberal Arts and Sciences. The Divisions may be divided into such departments as shall from time to time be recommended by the Executive Committee and authorized by the Board of Regents.

Sec. 33.03. Powers of the Governing Faculties. The governing faculty of each of the several Divisions shall be in charge of the affairs of the Division, except to the extent that such affairs are hereinafter placed in charge of the Dean and Executive Committee, and except that originally and until such time as the Executive Committee shall recommend and the Board of Regents shall authorize, the functions and responsibilities of the several governing faculties shall be discharged as provided in Section 33.04, below. The governing faculty of each Division shall provide the necessary courses of instruction, prepare suitable requirements for admission, proper curriculums, and appropriate requirements for graduation, which shall become effective upon approval by the Board of Regents. The governing faculties shall recommend to the Board candidates for degrees, and shall exercise such other powers as are ordinarily exercised by school or college governing faculties.

Sec. 33.04. Standing Committees. A standing committee shall be created for each Division established in the Dearborn Center. Until such time as may be determined, the standing committee shall represent the faculty of the Division. It shall perform those functions and discharge those responsibilities ordinarily vested in governing faculties, and shall stand in the same relationship to the Dean and Executive Committee of the Dearborn Center as does a governing faculty in discharge of its functions and responsibilities.

Each standing committee shall consist of such members of the University Senate as shall be designated by the President. The members shall serve for terms of one year and shall be eligible for reappointment.

Sec. 33.05. The Dean and the Executive Committee. The executive functions of the Dearborn Center shall be performed by a Dean assisted by an Executive Committee. The Executive Committee shall consist of the

Dean of the Dearborn Center, the deans of the corresponding schools and colleges on the Ann Arbor campus or their designated alternates, and three members of the University Senate to be appointed by the Board of Regents on recommendation of the President. The appointed members shall hold office for three years. The terms shall be so adjusted that one shall expire each year. The Dean of the Dearborn Center shall be Chairman of the Executive Committee.

The Executive Committee is charged with the duty of investigating and formulating educational, research, and instructional policies for consideration by the faculties of the several Divisions, and it shall act for the Center in matters related to the budget, promotions, appointments, plant extensions, and all other financial affairs.

The Dean shall perform such functions and assume such responsibilities for the administration of business and financial affairs, student activities, etc., as may from time to time be designated by the President and the Board of Regents.

Sec. 33.06. Graduate Instruction. Any one of the several Divisions may be authorized to offer graduate instruction leading to the Master's Degree, but no such program of graduate studies may be authorized except in compliance with the rules and regulations covering similar offerings on the Ann Arbor campus. Unless specifically excepted, such offerings shall be under the general jurisdiction of the Dean and the Executive Board of the Horace H. Rackham School of Graduate Studies.

Appendix 2.7: Recommendations of Balzhiser Committee, May 1969 (from the Dearborn Campus Planning Committee Study Report)

In support of this broad recommendation, the Committee makes the following specific recommendations:

1. Academic programs at Dearborn should be directed toward the needs of the western Detroit metropolitan area, and should consider specifically the needs of urban youth, local public service agencies and institutions and local industry. Special attention should be given to innovation in developing programs to meet these needs.

2. Dearborn should offer four year academic programs in the liberal arts and sciences, education, business administration, and engineering. It should continue its present cooperative programs but on an optional basis rather than as a requirement, and it should create additional areas for cooperative programs within the Literature, Science and the Arts Division.

3. Master's level programs should be initiated where faculty strengths and resources permit without distracting from the development of undergraduate options. Graduate programs should be given under the general supervision of the Rackham School of Graduate Studies and the direct supervision of a director of graduate studies on the Dearborn Campus. The director should also serve as Associate Dean of the Rackham School and be a voting member of the Executive Board. A Dearborn Graduate Board should be established to plan the orderly development of graduate programs on the Campus. Initial composition should include three members of the Dearborn faculty and three members of the Ann Arbor graduate faculty with the Ann Arbor members phased out over a three year period.

4. The name of the Campus should be chosen to connote the autonomy of the Campus and facilitate its future transition to independent status. Yet it should indicate that, like the Ann Arbor Campus, it is presently governed by the Regents of The University of Michigan through the President and Executive Officers. The present designation "The University of Michigan Dearborn Campus" could be continued during the developmental period.

5. The chief executive officer of the Campus should report to the President and other executive officers of The University. He should carry a title other than "Dean" (perhaps Provost or Chancellor) to allow him flexibility in internally structuring the Campus.

6. The Dearborn Campus should be advised by a citizens' committee appointed by the Board of Regents and broadly representative of the metropolitan area.

7. The Campus should plan for growth to 5,000 full-time students by 1980. The five year development phase should bring the Campus to a level of 2,200 students.

8. A capital building program should be initiated at once. The most urgent needs are:
   a) A new library building,
   b) Student activities facilities,
   c) Additional campus housing.

9. A long-range plan for campus physical development should be undertaken that will provide for the projected enrollment.

Appendix 2.8: Regents Approval of Expansion for UM-D

U. of M. Regents Minutes, November 1969

In conjunction with the appointment of Vice-President Spurr (p. 217), the President proposed that the following amended recommendations concerning the Flint and Dearborn report be approved:

Flint and Dearborn Report Recommendations Approved

1. That the University commit itself to the continued support of a strong four-year undergraduate program at Flint, and the expansion of the Dearborn program to a full four-year undergraduate program. In making this recommendation, it is understood that there are special difficulties in this respect at Dearborn, that there are many sensitivities involved, and that care must be taken to proceed amicably. The question of spin-off for Dearborn should remain open for the time being.
2. That the University proceed to develop master's level programs where appropriate and justified at each campus, and that phased steps to place these programs under local control be taken as quickly as possible, on terms to be developed jointly with the Rackham School.
3. That the separate budget status of Dearborn be acknowledged, and that a gradually phased move toward the same status for Flint be undertaken.
4. That, as developments warrant, the University move towards a chancellor system at Flint and Dearborn subject to two qualifications: (1) that faculty and student representatives be afforded an opportunity to participate in the process of choosing a chancellor, and (2) that the retirement at 65 rule, presently in effect for Executive Officers on the Ann Arbor campus, be applied to chancellors.
5. That the administrative relationship of the two branch campuses to Ann Arbor be re-examined, with a view towards: (1) providing more time and attention from the University administration to assist in the solutions of the development of the branch campuses, and (2) maximizing the potential interrelationships in administrative and educational areas to achieve both quality and economy. (Specifically, high-cost, low enrollment courses at the two campuses should not be offered without exploring the potential for providing such educational service out of Ann Arbor. Likewise, computer, TV, and other services from Ann Arbor should be exploited.)
6. That in the development of educational programs at the two campuses, neither be committed to traditional departmental or college lines and that emphasis be placed upon innovative programs particularly related to area and community problems.
7. That similar cognizance of the educational programs and the educational needs of the geographic area served be taken in the development of admissions standards and practices.
8. That within these general guidelines, the Executive Officers proceed with the implementation of the Study Reports.

Approval was given to the above recommendations.

All of the above actions were by unanimous vote except where indicated.

Appendix 2.9a: Regents Approval of New UM-D Structure

U. of M. Regents Minutes, May 1973

UM-Dearborn
Bylaws Approved

The Regents approved the proposed new Bylaws for The University of Michigan-Dearborn submitted by Chancellor Goodall.

Appendix 2.9b: New Structure for UM-D

UM-D Bylaws—March 1973
ARTICLE VIII

THE INSTRUCTIONAL AND PROGRAMATIC UNITS

1. Schools and Colleges
The faculties offering degree programs may be organized into schools and colleges for the purpose of 1) providing instruction; 2) conducting scholarly investigations and research in those branches of knowledge that form the basis of modern culture, professional practice, and leadership in education, business, and industry; 3) applying this knowledge to the solution of problems of our society.

2. Governing Bodies
The management of the affairs of schools and colleges, subject to regental approval, is placed in the governing faculties, the deans, and the executive committees.

3. Departments
Subdivisions of a school or college under an administrative head maintained for the purpose of conducting a curriculum or curricula in a specified array of disciplines, may be organized into departments. Each department shall be organized in a manner to provide general participation by faculty members in the management of departmental affairs.

4. Divisions
A division may be established by the Board of Regents, upon the recommendation of the President and Chancellor, for the purpose of initiating and offering interdisciplinary and experimental degrees and other programs. A division may be under the direct supervision of the chief academic officer of the campus. It shall constitute a means of funding and administering instructional, research, and service programs that may involve members of the faculties of more than one school or college.

5. The Faculty of Each School or College
Each school or college faculty shall adopt rules for its own internal governance and shall appoint a secretary, define his duties and keep a record of faculty action.

In the absence of specific rules to the contrary, the rules of parlimentary procedure as described in *Robert's Rules of Order* shall be followed by the school and college faculties committees, boards, and other deliverative bodies.

6. Faculty Communications to the Board of Regents
Each faculty shall submit its communications to the Board of Regents in writing through the Chancellor and the President of the University. The Chancellor shall endorse Faculty communications, making explanatory statements as needed.

7. Bylaws of the Schools and Colleges
The Faculty of each School and College shall adopt bylaws and such further rules as it deems necessary for its own internal governance. Schools and College bylaws and rules shall be consonant with university and campus bylaws and shall be filed with the faculty secretary and made generally available to all members of the campus faculty.

Appendix 2.10: 1983 Statement of Mission and Purposes

MISSION AND PURPOSES OF THE UNIVERSITY OF MICHIGAN-DEARBORN

The University of Michigan-Dearborn is a regional campus of the University of Michigan and is committed to the University's tradition of excellence in teaching and research. As a regional center of learning, it brings distinguished teaching to commuter students from the surrounding business and industrial communities of metropolitan Detroit. Its mission encompasses three goals: (1) to examine, transmit, and expand the established knowledge of the liberal arts and the selected professions of education, engineering, and management; (2) to encourage students to develop a capacity to examine the world around them criticallys in professional fields or disciplines of the liberal arts.

To fulfill its mission, the University of Michigan-Dearborn is committed to the following purposes:

1) To maintain, as its first priority, a high quality of academic programs, instruction, faculty, and research activities. Its major emphasis will continue to be on an excellent set of undergraduate programs, but selected graduate programs at the master's level, reflective of the scholarly expertise of the faculty and of student needs, will complement the undergraduate programs. Specially designed interdisciplinary programs of study will continue to be offered at both the undergraduate and graduate levels.

2) To attract and accommodate a highly qualified and pluralistic student body, drawn from a variety of ethnic, social, and economic backgrounds, and to make a special effort to provide access to the campus's educational opportunities for non-traditional students.

3) To maintain and strengthen the ties of the University of Michigan-Dearborn with the industrial, business, civic and educational world around it. This effort involves (a) encouraging students to take advantage of off-campus learning and work experiences which complement and enhance traditional academic programs, such as cooperative work/study, internships, and directed teaching; and (b) encouraging faculty to participate in a constructive exchange of ideas and values related to human and environmental problems with those involved in non-academic areas of activity.

(Adopted by Faculty Advisory Committee on Campus Affairs, April 1983)

Appendix Three

Chronology of Events and People in the History of UM-D, 1955-1984

Note: High points in the history of UM-D marked with an asterisk.

1955—Explorations of Ford Motor Co. Training Director A. Pearson & staff concerning professional manpower supply.

January 11, 1956—Report by Pearson to Ford Motor Co. Administration Committee on "Company's long range needs for technical and professional employees"; appointment of a Special Committee to "develop a plan in cooperation with the University of Michigan."

January-June, 1956—UM prepares and presents to FMC the specifications and estimated cost for a campus such as that desired by FMC.

July 28, 1956—Special Committee makes specific recommendation for establishment of a Dearborn Center of UM, at capital cost of $6.5 million.

*December 17, 1956—Ford Gift announced at Fair Lane Mansion

January 9-10, 1957—Joint legislative statement urging UM to accept Ford gift.

January 11, 1957—Firms employed to study site and building development of land around Fair Lane.

*February 10, 1957—UM Regents officially accept Ford gift, authorize establishment of UM-D Center.

*June 13, 1957—LSA Committee (Walker) reports alone on UM-D Center plans.

July 12, 1957—UM Regents approve architect's plan for UM-D Center buildings; Hubbell, Roth, & Clark designated as site developers, Giffels & Vallet, Inc. of Detroit as architects.

*October 1, 1957—Deed to Fair Lane transferred to U.M. (202.59 acres).

*November 7, 1957—Dorr Committee recommends for academic and and administrative structure of UM-DC.

*January 10, 1958—UM Regents approve section of bylaws relating to UM-DC.

February 21, 1958—Utilities contracted for with City of Dearborn.

April 1958—Spence Bros. of Saginaw: general contract for construction of UM-D Center.

*May 22, 1958—Construction begins on UM-D Center.

*October 1, 1958—Stirton appointed director of UM-D Center.

October 1958—Agreement between UM and City of Dearborn on rates for city services to UM-D Center (water, sewage, police, fire department).

*March 1959—First Executive Committee appointed for UM-D Center.

March 23, 1959—Limited opening announced for UM-D Center.

*September 28, 1959—First regular term (quarter) begins at UM-D Center.

November 1959—Decision made to change from quarters to trimesters.

January 14, 1960—Liberal arts announced to begin in fall, 1960.

February 8, 1960—Second term (trimester) begins at UM-D Center.

March 2, 1960—Teacher education certification program announced for the fall, 1960.

March 16, 1960—Electrical Engineering Program announced for fall, 1960.

April 10, 1960—Open house for community at UM-D Center.

June, 1960—Religious Center established for HFCC and UM-D Center.

*Fall term, 1960—LSA Division, teacher education, and electrical engineering begun.

January 19, 1961—"Fair Lane Chorale" begun with Maynard Klein.

February 13, 1961—Evening M.B.A. from Ann Arbor School of Business Administration begun at UM-DC.

May 15, 1961—Conference at Fair Lane to decide use of mansion (Toynbee et al).

*October 20, 1961—Dedication ceremony for UM-D Center.

Fall term, 1961—Engineering math program begun.

January 1962—First UM-DC student newspaper, *The Fairlane* (January-May, 1962).

*January 20, 1962—First 14 graduates from UM-D Center (Ann Arbor ceremony).

*February 22, 1962—Trial co-op in liberal arts announced by Stirton.

April 1962—"Joint Committee for Institutional Cooperation" (UMDC and HFCC).

May, 1962—Boy, 13, drowned in lake.

*October 11, 1962—First graduation ceremony at UM-D Center (at Fair Lane)—20 graduates.

December 6, 1962—four point program of Religious Center announced (DeW. Baldwin).

*March 15, 1963—Name of Campus changed to U. of M., Dearborn Campus.

March 15, 1963—Committee for Development of Fair Lane established to raise $250,000.

June 1963—Women's committee for Fair Lane established to raise money for refurbishment of Fair Lane house and grounds. (Disbanded officially in June 1968 because of disagreement with U.M. on use of money raised.) Conducted tours of mansion in 1963-64.

June, 1963—first summer classes in LSA.

*September 1963—Graduate program in mechanical engineering announced, to begin in February 1964.

November 1963—Second UM-D Campus student newspaper, *Dearborn Wolverine* (went from November 1963—January 1964).

February 26, 1964—Stirton refutes rumors that UM-D Campus may expand to four years. President Hatcher reaffirms on February 28.

March/April 1964—Controversy over appointment of joint religious coordinator for UM-D Campus and HFCC.

September 1964—Center for Urban Studies established.

December 21, 1964—First issue of *Ad Hoc* (student newspaper to May 1967).

December 31, 1964—Donald Vincent leaves as head librarian.

March 29, 1965—Hatcher calls UM-D "inspearable part" of UM *(Ad Hoc, April 1)*.

March/April 1965—Plans to brick in courtyard pond dropped.

April 21, 1965—Stirton affirms continuance of Campus as upper division and graduate.

August 1965—George Baker, plant and grounds, left UM-D.

Fall 1965—TALUS funded ($1,000,000) for Center for Urban Studies.

Fall 1965—SGC constitution revised to broaden student representation.

October 13, 1965—*Ad Hoc* mentions natural science and social science co-op students.

February 1, 1966—Donald Klaasen becomes business manager of UM-D Campus.

March 23, 1966—John Dempsey announced candidacy for 16th Congressional seat.

April 1966—Eugene Kuthy leaves as business administration co-op coordinator.

Fall 1966—LSA Pass/Fail option introduced.

*May 18, 1967—Fair Lane made a National Historical Landmark.

May 26, 1967—Last issue of *Ad Hoc* until 10/27/69.

May 1967—Polk, Haithcox, Trauger, Cohen (faculty) leave UM-D.

June/July, 1967—Fair Lane Festival (music) on Fair Lane patio and lawn.

Fall 1967—C. Edward Wall made head librarian.

September 1967—Ecumenical Ministry to Higher Edfucation in Dearborn (EMHED) established.

June 20, 1968—Women of Fair Lane officially disbanded; "Ram" gift given.

July 5, 1968—Co-op for all three divisions mentioned in *Time* advertisement.

Summer 1968—Stirton retires; Norman Scott made dean of UM-D Campus.

October 1968—Burton Harrison, assistant to chief executive officer, hired.

January 1969—Richard Reynolds becomes director of university relations.

April 18, 1969—First of "Evenings at Fair Lane" arranged by UM Alumni of Dearborn (Iris Becker, chairperson of "Evenings").

*May 1969—Balzhiser Committee (Dearborn Campus Planning Study Committee) report.

Summer 1969—Hertzler's "Association of Community College Biologists" begun.

Summer 1969—Myron Simon leaves for University of California-Irvine.

Summer 1969—Allan Emery leaves for U of M Computing Center.

Fall 1969—Paul Carter appointed first UM-D director of graduate studies.

Fall 1969—Athletic pad built; Rudy Radulovich appointed first director of intramural and recreational sports.

November 11, 1969—Tenth Anniversary celebration of UM-D.

*November 21, 1969—Regents approve expansion of UM-D to first two years.

November 1969—Stephen Spurr appointed to oversee expansion at UM-D and UM-F.

November 23, 1969—Governor Milliken visits UM-D Campus.

December 1969/January 1970—Clash between state Board of Education and Regents on branch campus.

*January, 1970—B.G.S. implemented in LSA (to by-pass foreign language requirement).

*February 23, 1970—Legislative hearing at UM-D on "spin-off"; mock funeral.

May 12, 1970—Chancellor Selection Committee has first meeting.

Summer 1970—Articulation projects in math and science with community colleges.

July 9, 1970—Legislature approrpiates $225,000 for UM-D expansion (first money).

June, 1970—UM-D opposes extension of Gildow by Ford Development.

July 1, 1970—Oakland University separated from MSU.

*August 1970—First NCA accreditation of UM-D independent of Ann Arbor.

August 20, 1970—Scott says limited number of liberal arts co-op jobs available *(Dearborn Press)*.

Fall 1970—Robert Smock appointed academic coordinator.

October 1, 1970—Fleming appoints citizens' commission to study campus and community.

*October 18, 1970—First concert of Fair Lane Music Guild.

October 1970—Jack Petosky appointed as first separate director of admissions.

December 9-10, 1970—"Black Awareness" days at UM-D.

January 1971—Enrollment goal of 10,000 by 1980 becomes common statement.

*February 1971—Electrical engineering master's degree begun at UM-D.

February 25, 1971—Robert H. Maier announced as first UM-D chancellor.

Winter 1971—Child Care Center begun in Fair Lane (moved to cottages next year).

*April 1971—"University of Michigan-Dearborn" adopted as campus name.

May 1971—Robert Maier resigns as chancellor.

May 1971—Rudy Radulovich (director of intramural sports) died.

*June 1971—Leonard E. Goodall appointed chancellor.

*July 1971—First official legislative appropriation to UM-D as line item.

Summer 1971—First summer science workshop for high school teachers (Gelderloos).

Summer 1971—Calvin DeWitt leaves for University of Wisconsin.

August 1971—First full-time counselors appointed (Brown and McAllister).

August 1971—Howard Conlon appointed as assistant to chancellor for planning.

September 1971—Bernard Klein appointed Professor and director of Center for Urban Studies.

Appendix Three   93

*Fall 1971—First freshman class of 313 enrolls; total enrollment of 1,369 (50 percent increase).
*Fall 1971—Political science internship program begun by Walter DeVries.
October 1971—Richard Sypula appointed director of intramural and recreational sports.
October 1971—Search Committee for dean of academic affairs appointed.
December 1971—UM-D trades land with Archdiocese: for building Gabriel Richard Center.
January 23, 1972—Goodall officially installed as first chancellor (ceremony).
March 1972—Funds approved for COB; not appropriated until June 8, 1972.
March 25, 1972—Metro Science Fair at UM-D
June 8, 1972—Michigan Senate appropriates planning money for library and athletic building.
*July 1972—Eugene Arden appointed as first dean of academic affairs.
*Fall 1972—Professional Development in Engineering Degree program begun.
Fall 1972—Enrollment of 1,977.
Fall 1972—Association of Women Students formed.
Fall 1972—Dahlke begins Keller Plan for Calculus 1.
September 1972—Joseph Wright appointed as director of student affairs.
October 1972—"Industrial Engineering" changed to Industrial & Systems Engineering.
November 9, 1972—Ruth Shafer appointed first director of Financial Aid Office.
January 10, 1973—Classroom and Office Building (COB) opened.
February 1973—David McAllister appointed as director of special projects.
*March 27, 1973—New bylaws and campus structure approved by Faculty Congress.
May 1973—Safety and Security Office established under George Gilbert.
June 8, 1973—Legislative planning money voted for Library, COB, and athletic building.
*June 1973—First modular units set up, attached to SAB.
*June 1973—Gabriel Richard Center finished.
*June 1973—New academic units announced (CASL, etc.); IDS still being formed.
July 1973—Regents approve addition (later called ROC) to SAB.
Summer 1973—Donald Klaasen leaves UM-D; Hadley Schaefer leaves for Stanford University.
September 21, 1973—Regents request Wayne County Road Commission not to extend Hines Drive.
*September 1973—Master of Management Degree begun.
Fall 1973—Dick Perry appointed first fencing coach (left in 1980).
Fall 1973—Separate Personnel Office first established (Douglas Geister).
Fall 1973—Number of evening courses doubled; simplified registration.
Fall 1973—Helen Graves takes over political science internship program.
*October 1973—First HEW grant for CASL co-op program announced ($25,000).
*November 22, 1973—$19 million expansion for UM-D announced.
*November 1973—First Board of UM-D Alumni Society elected.
February 1974—Early childhood education program started.
February 1974—Symposium on "Creativity in the Academy."
February 1974—Richard Schwartz appointed director of business affairs.
March 1974—Arden's title changed to Provost.
Spring 1974—UM-D Women's Commission established.
June 1974—Tours of Fair Lane taken up again after eight year hiatus.
*June 1974—Individualized Learning courses begun under Lilly grant.
June 1974—Regents approve five-year capital development plan, including library.
*July 26, 1974—Exchange of land with Ford Development Co. (Mercury & Gildow).
*Summer 1974—NCA accreditation renewed for 10 years.
September 1974—Felix Barthelemy appointed director of personnel.
September 1974—First varsity sport begun: soccer, Van Dimitriou as coach (to 1978).
September 4, 1974—UM-D Role Statement approved by Regents; 13 goals.
September 13, 1974—Fifteenth Anniversary celebration.

Fall 1974—First women's varsity basketball team (John Langford, coach).

Fall 1974—Core Curriculum Review Committee at work.

Fall 1974—Parking reciprocity established with Ann Arbor campus.

Fall 1974—Initiation of program for nursing students from Henry Ford Hospital.

Fall 1974—Alburey Castell first appointed as visiting professor of philosophy.

October 1974—Goodall first objects to projected budget cuts.

*October 12, 1974—First Renaissance English literature conference at Fair Lane (Pebworth & Summers).

November 1974—UM-D Women's Commission elects first steering committee.

December 1974—Second CASL co-op grant announced ($30,000).

December 8, 1974—First drama performance by UM-D group *(Phoenix too Frequent)*.

December 11, 1974—Fire in Module 8.

January 1975—Betty Kaufman first coordinator of women's programs.

February 1975—Regents appropriate $773,000: renovations in Engineering Building (physics labs, lecture halls).

*March 1975—LIbrary and GILB excluded from state's capital funds appropriation.

March 1975—Major renovation study approved for Fair Lane (Report in January 1976).

*March 1975—Lee Katz appointed associate dean for development and evening program.

Spring 1975—NEH grant for American studies courses/Henry Ford Museum (Berkove).

June 1975—ROC finished (but not named until Feb. 1976).

*September 1975—M.A. in Education Degree begun.

September 1975—IGNITE program for high school students first implemented at UM-D.

September 1975—Degrees in Environmental Studies and Environmental Science begun.

September 1975—John Hicks appointed director of personnel.

September 1975—New concentration in anthropology (CASL).

*Fall 1975—School of Engineering programs receive first accreditation (ECPD) separate from UM-AA.

Fall 1975—Cross country track squad organized (Tony Mifsud, until 1980).

Fall 1975—First 2+2 program: in management with Henry Ford Community College.

Fall 1975—Professional Development Degree programs begun in CASL and Urban Education.

Fall 1975—Long Range Planning Committee established under Provost Arden.

Fall 1975—First varsity hockey team (coached by Richard Sypula).

Fall and Winter 1975-76—cooperative program with WSU's college of Lifelong Learning.

October 1975—Parking structure authorized; to be finished September 1976.

*November 1975—Official acknowledgment that major building program was stalled.

November 1975—First public Natural Area trail guide brochure made available

November 1975—Medical service for UM-D contracted with Henry Ford Hospital—Fairlane Center.

December 1975—First campus teaching awards made.

December 1975—Renovations to Engineering Building finished for use in winter term.

January 1976—Ewald Seiter's purple martin bird house put in Jensen's Meadow.

January 15, 1976—Regents balk at funding recommended renovations of Fair Lane ($6.4 million).

February 18, 1976—Al Obelsky died in Japan.

March 1976—Goodall discusses limited enrollment because of financial pinch.

April 1976—Goodall and Bundy present plan for joint performing arts center to Regents. (Henry Ford Community College went to its own plan in November 1976.)

Late 1970's cultural activities at UM-D, many at Fair Lane:

Wind Ensemble	Evenings at Fair Lane	Films
Choral Ensemble	Cultural Events Committee	Jazz concerts
Ann Parks, organ	concerts	Prominent speakers
Fair Lane Music Guild	Theater (improvisation and plays)	

April 1976—First Young Authors' Conference.

April 4, 1976—Bids authorized for athletic building.

June 1976—Eight hundred rose bushes planted by Fair Lane Rose Society.

July 21, 1976—Braille Trail opened at Fair Lane.

*July 1976—Title changes for Arden, Schwartz, and Wright.

August 1, 1976—La Janace Stone appointed director of financial aid.

August 1976—E. Hertzler conducts joint survey with unions on OIL courses.

August 1976—Regents approve architectural and cost study for student center (Mall).

*Fall 1976—Two new campus entrances off extended Evergreen opened.

Fall 1976—UM-D engineering and management courses offered at Birmingham Center for
  Continuing Education.

Fall 1976—Budget Priorities Committee begun.

Fall 1976—First issue of *Philosophy and Literature* (Dutton *et al*).

October 1976—Second Biennial Renaissance Literature Conference at Fair Lane.

October-November 1976—"Teach-in on Detroit" by Cultural Events Committee.

October 1976—Regents approve plans and bidding for athletic bldg. ("Phase 1").

November 1976—State Task Force recommends joint library *et al* for UM-D & HFCC.

November 1976—Performance of *When You Comin' Back Red Ryder?*

December 1976—Robert Behrens joins accounting staff.

January 1977—Goodall rejects Task Force recommendations on shared library with HFCC.

February 18, 1977—Regents approve revised UM-D Goal Statement.

*March 14, 1977—Kellogg grant to Hertzler for REACH ($205,000).

*March 18, 1977—Stirton professorship instituted by Regents.

March 1977—Glass recycling center permanently closed.

April 1977—The "Hinge" closes down.

April 15, 1977—Task Force on Faculty Concerns submits petition to President Fleming.

May 9, 1977—"Pool" restaurant at Fair Lane opened.

May 17, 1977—First Alumni Day at UM-D.

*May 20, 1977—Master of Public Administration Degree approved by Regents.

May 20, 1977—Regents approve dropping "Urban" from "Division of Urban Education."

May 1977—UM-D helps form Mid-Central Collegiate Hockey Association.

May 1977—Paul Carter retires.

July 13, 1977—Gift of $10,700 from Ford Motor Co. for natural area brochures, tapes.

Summer 1977—Washington Intern Program begun.

Summer 1977—Toronto Political Science Intern Program begun.

Summer 1977—First of Marilynn Rosenthal's overseas courses on medical care systems.

Summer 1977—Margarette Eby left UM-D for University of Northern Iowa.

August 1977—Controversy over NOVA extension classes held at UM-D.

*Fall 1977—Project REACH officially begun.

Fall 1977—Sal Rinella appointed director of institutional analysis

September 1, 1977—CETA grant of $214,000 (worker training program).

1977-78—First annual UM-D fund raising drive.

September 1977—Elton Higgs appointed UM-D director of graduate studies.

October 6, 1977—UM-D athletic teams officially called "Wolves."

November 1977—Ed Bagale named director of admissions; Geitka director of computing services.

December 1977—Regents approve construction of University Mall.

January 1978—New "Hinge" coffeehouse opened in ROC (old one: 1967-77 in Fair Lane).

February 1978—Adray contributes $5,000 to outdoor athletic facilities.

March 25, 1978—Conference at UM-D on "The Power of the Hero."

March 31, 1978—Former President Gerald Ford visits UM-D.

*May 1978—First regular Regents' meeting at Fair Lane.

June 1978—Bids on Library, construction of Mall for July approved.

Summer 1978—Hardee's begins operation at UM-D.

August 1978—Richard Schwartz resigns; Rinella appointed acting vice-chancellor for business affairs.

*****Fall 1978**—Fieldhouse and Ice Arena opened.

*****Fall 1978**—Science Learning Center began operation (Orin Gelderloos).

September 1978—Peter Amann named first Stirton professor.

September 1978—Division of Education begins physical education courses.

September 1978—Second annual UM-D fundraising drive.

October 1978—Third Biennial Renaissance Literature Conference at Fair Lane.

October 1978—Powerhouse restored to operation (defunct since 1950).

October 17, 1978—Ground-breaking for Library

November 1978—Dearborn Round Table established by Goodall *et al.*

December 8, 1978—Agreement between UM-D and HFCC to mesh Associate Degree and B.G.S. ("2+2").

December 15, 1978—Sal Rinella appointed vice-chancellor for business affairs.

December 1978—UM-D Archives Committee established.

February 9-10, 1979—Fieldhouse and Ice Arena dedicated.

March 7, 1979—Diane Culp (Librarian) died (UM-D since '69; memorial glass March 31, 1983).

March 1979—$275,000 grant from Ford Motor Co. to establish undergraduate manufacturing engineering program.

*****April 1979**—Goodall announces departure from UM-D (end of June).

Spring 1979—NEH grant for courses in Society, Values, and Choice (Higgs).

Spring 1979—New concentrations: American Studies and Microbiology (CASL).

May 1979—First Susan B. Anthony Award, to Betty Kaufman.

May 1979—Chancellor Search Committee appointed.

Summer 1979—Modules on N.E. corner of campus moved away.

Summer 1979—Health Care Systems course visits Republic of China.

July 1, 1979—Bernard Klein becomes acting chancellor (until July 1980).

August 1979—Sam Namminga appointed director of Office of Institutional Analysis.

August 16, 1979—Carl Rasmussen (math) shot to death.

Fall 1979—First "Phonathon" fund-raiser.

Fall 1979—First mini-sabbaticals awarded.

*****Fall 1979**—M.S.E. in Industrial and Systems Engineering begun.

Fall 1979—Academic section of University Mall opened.

October 1979—Division of Education awarded $111,000 HEW grant.

November 1979—New concentrations: International Studies (CASL), Public Administration (IDS).

November 1979—Campus Writing Lab opened.

December 1979—Frances Cousens retires.

December 1979—Herschel Wallace retires.

January 1980—$10,000 from National Foundation for Minority Engineering Students.

March 1980—Virginia Sayles becomes UM-D director of extension.

March 1980—Third annual Math Track Meet.

April 1980—Fifth Young Authors' Conference.

May 1980—Alumni Fund Drive nets $11,140.

Spring 1980—The "Hinge" closes down second time.

*****July 1980**—William A. Jenkins becomes second chancellor.

Fall 1980—Change-over to computerized registration complete.

Fall 1980—New concentration in Manufacturing Engineering.

*****Fall 1980**—New Library opened on limited basis.

*****October 1980**—Commercial section of University Mall opens.

October 1980—Fourth Biennial Renaissance Literature Conference at Fair Lane.

December 1, 1980—Rhonnye Otuonye appointed first director of affirmative action.

January 1981—UM-D Extension Office separates from Ann Arbor.

*April 11, 1981—New Library dedicated; Terrence H. Bell, key speaker.

*April 1981—Distribution of $500,000 cut in UM-D base budget announced.

April 1981—Chancellor Jenkins notes possibility of salary cut to balance budget.

August 1981—Auburey Castell leaves UM-D.

Summer 1981—David Emerson leaves for University of Nevada-Las Vegas.

Fall 1981—Minority enrollment at UM-D reaches nine percent.

*Fall 1981—School of Engineering programs receive reaccreditation by ABET.

*September 1981—Regents appropriate raise of three percent for UM-D, six percent for UM-F and UM-AA.

*September 1981—M.B.A. Degree begun, to replace M.M. Degree.

September 1981—New concentration: Health and Society (IDS).

September 1981—Governor calls back $267,000 from 1981-82 UM-D budget.

September 1981—Francis Wayman becomes director of Division of Interdisciplinary Studies.

September 1981—Dennis Papazian appointed UM-D director of graduate studies.

September 8, 1981—Frances Cousens appointed director of affirmative action.

October 1981—Governor calls back another $299,403 from 1981-82 budget.

November 1981—Office of Individualized Learning becomes REACH.

December 1981—Thomas Schroth (engineering co-op coordinator) retires.

February 1982—Emmanuel Hertzler retires.

Spring 1982—UM-D hockey team finishes 23-6-1 season.

March 1982—Self-Study Steering Committee appointed for 1984 NCA evaluation.

April 1, 1982—Donn Werling appointed director of Henry Ford Estate-Fair Lane.

April 2, 1982—John Dempsey (former LSA Chairman) died.

May 1982—Annual Fund Campaign for 1981-82 nets $18,542.

May 1982—Soon Chung (math) killed in auto accident (UM-D since 1974).

June 1982—Susan Burt appointed director of academic development.

June 1982—Cut of $74,790, '81-82 and '82-83 UM-D budget; fourth in nine months.

September 1982—Edward Lumsdaine appointed dean of School of Engineering.

September 1982—Office of Academic Development becomes "Sponsored Research and Development."

October 1982—Chris Chetsanga receives $134,000 grant from National Cancer Institute.

October 1982—Fifth Biennial Renaissance Literature Conference at Fair Lane.

October 25-29, 1982—First 'Spirit Week' held by students.

Fall 1982—First REACH courses on local cable TV.

Fall 1982—Richard Axsom begins exhibit of Frank Stella prints.

Fall 1982—Army Officer Education Program (ROTC) reopened for men and women.

November 1982—Citizens Advisory Committee makes plea to Regents for UM-D support.

December 15, 1982—Fair Lane mansion named "Henry Ford Estate-Fair Lane."

January 1, 1983—Richard Morshead reappointed dean of Education (was associate dean).

March 3, 1983—William Stirton died.

March 1983—25th Anniversary Committee appointed.

March 24, 1983—First UM-D Honors Convocation.

March 31, 1983—Stained glass by V. Sattler hung in Library, for Diane Culp.

March/April 1983—Aviva Robinson paintings shown in Library.

April 1983—Governor calls back $375,000 from 1982-83 UM-D appropriation.

Spring 1983—First competition for Equipment and Research Incentive Awards.

May 1983—Annual Fund Campaign nets $20,000, up nine percent from 1981-82.

May 1983—William Agresti (I. & S. Engineering) leaves UM-D for industry.

June 1983—Christopher Chetsanga leaves for University of Zimbabwe (UM-D since 1972).

July 1983—Leslie Tentler given three-year commission to write history of Archdiocese.

July 1983—Burt Harrison retires.

July 1983—Guest Scholar program for senior citizens begun.

July 15, 1983—Regents approve inclusion of UM-D in "Campaign for Michigan."

Summer 1983—Preparations completed in Library for GEAC computer.

Summer 1983—Pit area in ROC filled in and covered.

September 9, 1983—Glass sculpture in honor of William Stirton contributed by Maccabees Mutual.

September 29, 1983—$15,000 in alumni pledges from phonathon.

Fall 1983—Richard Reynolds made director of alumni relations.

*Fall 1983—Minority enrollment at UM-D hits record 9.6 percent.

October 24-28, 1983—Second annual "Spirit Festival" (students).

October 25, 1983—Eric Bolling appointed director of affirmative action.

*January 1984—American Chemical Society recertifies UM-D chemistry program.

January 1984—Self-Study Report ready for NCA.

March 7-9, 1984—NCA accrediting team visits UM-D.

April 4, 1984—New Jensen's Meadow martin house to replace burned one.

April 1984—Office of Institutional Analysis becomes Office of Institutional Research.

May 1984—Annual Young Authors' Conference.

May 1984—Annual Fund Campaign for '83-'84 nets $34,239.

*May 24, 1984—Ford Motor Co. gives $800,000 for Computer Aided Engineering Laboratory.

June 1984—Dale Chihuly glass creations shown in Library.

July 1984—Denis Dutton leaves UM-D for University of Canterbury, New Zealand.

July 1984—Sal Rinella resigns as vice-chancellor for business affairs; Behrens appointed.

*July 1984—NCA accreditation renewed until 1994.

*July 1984—UM-D staff: extra three percent (total eight percent) in salary raise for '84-'85.

*July 1984—13.2 percent increase in legislative appropriation for 1984-85.

July 1984—John Potts (physics) leaves UM-D for industry job.

August 1984—Edward Wall resigns as director of Library; Shirley Smith appointed.

August 1984—Barbara Forisha-Kovach leaves UM-D for Rutgers-New Brunswick.

September 1984—First Communiversity Open House held.

September 1984—Tsung-Yen Na (Engin.) appointed Stirton Professor for 1984-1989.

September 28, 1984—Founders' Day Luncheon on 25th Anniversary of first class.

*Fall 1984—School of Engineering programs receive reaccreditation by ABET.

Appendix Four

Selected Tables of UM-D Personnel
and Units, 1959-1984

1. Original UM-D Faculty (Fall 1959-Fall 1960)

A. Fall 1959 and Early 1960

Business Administration
D. Ross Cowan, John G. Hutchinson, Hadley Schaeffer, Joseph Crafton

Engineering
Howard Colby, John F. Barrows, C.W. Johnson, Paul Trojan (1960), Robert E.A. Little

Literature, Science, and the Arts
Sidney Warchausky, Chester Camp, Emmanuel Hertzler (1960)

B. Fall 1960

Business Administration
Cedric Fricke

Literature, Science, and the Arts
David Burks, Paul Carter, Carl Cohen, John Dempsey, Allan Emery, Loren Findlayson, Fred Goodman, Carl Haag, Alvan Obelsky

2. First UM-D Administrators

A. Campus Level
William E. Stirton, Director of the Dearborn Center
Herschel L. Wallace, Director of Student Services
Robert W. Beecher, Business Manager
Donald E. Vincent, Director of Library Services
Robert E.A. Little, Engineering Coordinator
L. Joseph Crafton, Bus. Ad. Coordinator

B. Division Chairs (based in Ann Arbor)
R. Lee Brummet, Business Administration
Axel Marin, Engineering
Karl Litzenberg, Literature, Science and the Arts

3. First UM-D Professional/Administrative Staff

Lee Miglio, Executive Secretary and Assistant to Chief Executive Officer (1959-).
George Baker, Manager of Plant and Grounds (1959-1965).
Gene Monier, Assistant Manager of Plant and Grounds (1959-81).
Peter Murphy, Security Officer (1959-).
Donald Haidys, Plant and Engineering (1959-).

4. Original Academic Programs (Fall 1959-Fall 1960)

Fall 1959
Bachelor of Business Administration (courses in business administration, accounting, finance, industrial relations, management, marketing, and statistics)

Bachelor of Science in Engineering
Industrial Engineering
Mechanical Engineering (courses in Chem. and Met. Eng., Elec. Eng., Eng. Mech., Ind. Eng., Math, and Mech. Eng.)

Fall 1960
Bachelor of Arts and Bachelor of Science
Biological Sciences
Chemistry
Economics
English
History
Mathematics
Psychology and Sociology
(also courses in French, Philosophy, Political Science)

5. Academic Units, 1959-1984

Division of Business Administration, 1959; became the School of Management, 1971.

Division of Engineering, 1959; became the School of Engineering, 1971.

Division of Literature, Science, and the Arts, 1960; became the College of Arts, Sciences, and Letters, 1971.

Division of Urban Education, 1971; became the Division of Education, 1977.

Division of Interdisciplinary Studies, 1974.

6. Permanent Buildings, 1959-1984

1959: Classroom and Administration Building
Faculty Office Building
Engineering Building
Student Activities Building (including Library)

1972: Classroom and Office Building

1975: Recreation and Organizations Center

1976: Parking Structure

1978: Fieldhouse/Ice Arena

1979: University Mall

1980: Library Building

7. Heads of UM-D Campus-Wide Units, 1959-1984

A. Chief Executive Officers
William E. Stirton, October 1958-August 1968
Norman Scott, September 1968-July 1971
Leonard E. Goodall, August 1971-June 1979
Bernard Klein, July 1979-June 1980
William A. Jenkins, July 1980-

B. Chief Academic Officers
Robert Smock, Academic Coordinator, 1970-1972
Eugene Arden, Dean of Academic Affairs, 1972-1974; Provost, 1974-1979; Vice-Chancellor for Academic Affairs, 1979-

C. Head Librarians
Donald Vincent, 1959-1964
Lynn Bartlett, 1964-65
Harold Young, 1965-66
Donald Dennis, 1966-68
Edward Wall, 1968-1984

D. Chief Business Officers
Robert Beecher, 1959-1965
Donald Klaasen, 1965-1973
Richard Schwartz, 1973-1978
Sal Rinella, 1978-1984

E. Student Affairs Directors
Herschel Wallace, 1959-1971; Director of Registration and Records, 1971-1979
Joseph Wright, 1971-1976; Dean of Students, 1976-present

8. Heads of UM-D Academic Units (former names of units in parentheses), 1959-1984

A. School of Engineering (Division of Engineering)
Axel Marin, 1959-1963 (Marin and Trojan co-chairs, 63-64)
Paul Trojan, 1963-1964
Robert Cairns, 1963-1980
Paul Trojan, 1980-1982
Edward Lumsdaine, 1982-

B. School of Management (Division of Business Administration)
R. Lee Brummett, 1959-1963
L. Joseph Crafton, 1963-1965
Hadley P. Schaefer, 1965-1969
A. Richard Krachenberg, 1969-71
D. Ross Cowan, 1971-73 [Chairman]; 1973-1975 [Acting Dean]
A. Richard Krachenberg, 1975-76 [Acting Dean]
William R.D. Martin, 1976-1985

C. College of Arts, Sciences, and Letters (Division of Literature, Science, and the Arts)
Karl Litzenburg, 1959-1965
John Dempsey, 1965-1968
David Emerson, 1968-1969
Dennis Papazian, 1969-1973
Elton Higgs, 1973-1974 [Acting Dean]
Joachim Bruhn, 1974-1979
David Emerson, 1979-1981
Eugene Grewe, 1981-1983 [Interim Dean]
Victor Wong, 1983-

D. **Division of Education (Teaching Certification Program, Department of Education)**
Paul Carter, 1960-1970
Richard Morshead, 1970-

E. **Division of Interdisciplinary Studies**
Francis W. Wayman, Jr., 1976-

9. **Recipients of Campus Distinguished Teaching Awards, 1975-1985**

1975-76
Peter Amann
Helen Graves

1976-77
James W. Brown
Sidney M. Bolkosky

1977-78
Elias Baumgarten
Donald Proctor
Swatantra Kachhal

1978-79
Richard E. Czarnecki
John F. Devlin

1979-80
Carolyn Kraus

1980-81
Richard Moyer
Bette Kreuz

1981-82
Orin Gelderloos
Richard Straub

1982-83
David James
Seyed Shahidepour

1983-84
Patrick Dobel
Michael LaChance

1984-85
Dorothy Lee
Elaine Clark

10. **Student Government Presidents, 1961-1984**

Bud Hebets, 1961-62
John A. Scott, 1962-63
John Anderson, 1963-64
Ronald Moore, Fall 1964
Thomas Goebel, Spring 1965
John Bambery, Summer 1965
Hal Denton, Fall 1965
James Lovett, Winter 1966
William Goodwin, Summer 1966
Douglas Grubbe, Fall 1966
James Geisler, Winter 1967

Bruce Whitaker, Fall 1967
Neil Kuschner, Winter 1968
Brian Marzek, Fall 1968
Stuart Caulfield, Winter 1969
Eugene Valentine, Fall 1969
James Vandenbousch, Winter 1970
Richard Sypula, Fall 1970
Valerie Pazzanese (Boguslawski), Winter 1971
Thomas Mosely, November 1972 to March 1973
Pam Hodges (Porter), March 1973 to October 1973
Jerome Arcy, October 1973 to March 1974
Kent Aitchinson, March 1974 to September 1974
David Sanders, September 1974 to March 1975
Harvey Altus, 1975-76
Joe Stevens, 1976-77
Bruce Templeton, 1977-78
William Runco, 1978-79
David Hopkins, 1979-80
Saul Anuzis, 1980-81
David Yesh, 1981-82
Eugene Palmer, 1982-83
William Dorotinsky, 1983-84
Thomas Byrne, 1984-85

11. Table of UM-D Enrollments and Budgets, 1959-60 through 1983-84*

	Enrollments (Fall Headcount)	Degrees Granted	Budgets
1959-60	34	none	$ 350,000
1960-61	211	none	310,665
1961-62	328	34	502,665
1962-63	481	122	627,672
1963-64	577	124	681,690
1964-65	643	210	772,774
1965-66	653	220	948,308
1966-67	703	243	1,222,932
1967-68	745	223	1,293,806
1968-69	770	240	1,414,285
1969-70	915	245	2,311,734
1970-71	896	294	2,746,055
1971-72	1,367	335	3,681,424
1972-73	1,978	365	4,982,620
1973-74	2,938	378	6,179,030
1974-75	4,298	442	7,941,500
1975-76	4,858	556	9,029,900
1976-77	5,275	563	10,347,545
1977-78	5,480	637	11,432,200
1978-79	5,957	768	12,956,200
1979-80	6,400	792	14,607,300
1980-81	6,360	818	16,220,300
1981-82	6,575	866	16,950,916
1982-83	6,390	961	18,221,000
1983-84	6,399	932	19,763,000

*Source: UM-D Office of Institutional Research.

Edited by Marlene Goldsmith
Designed by B. Hay
Composed by Alpha 21 Typographers, Detroit, in ITC New Baskerville
Printed by Braun-Brumfield, Inc., Ann Arbor, on Glatco Matte Text
Bound by Braun-Brumfield, Inc. with Holliston Roxite Linen